Welcoming
Community

Welcoming Community

Diversity That Works

DOUGLAS AVILESBERNAL
with LINDA TRIEMSTRA COOK

J. DWIGHT STINNETT, SERIES EDITOR

Living Church

JUDSON PRESS
PUBLISHERS SINCE 1824

Join our mailing list for updates and special offers.
www.judsonpress.com/mailing_list.cfm

Welcoming Community: Diversity That Works

Interior design by Wendy Ronga, Hampton Design Group. Cover design by Tobias Becker and Birdbox Graphic Design (www.birdboxdesign.com).

Library of Congress Cataloging-in-Publication data
Avilesbernal, Douglas.
Welcoming community : diversity that works / Douglas Avilesbernal. — First [edition].
pages cm. — (Living church series)
ISBN 978-0-8170-1764-4 (pbk.: alk. paper) 1. Communities—Religious aspects—Christianity. 2. Church and minorities. I. Title.
BV625.A95 2015
254'.5—dc23   2015004050

Printed in the U.S.A.
First printing, 2016.

Contents

Preface to the Series

"What happened? Just a few years ago we were a strong church. We had thriving ministries and supported a worldwide mission effort. Our community knew us and cared about what we did. Now we're not sure if we can survive another year."

It is a painful conversation I have had with more church leaders than I can name here.

I explained how images such as *meltdown, tsunami, earthquake*, and *storm* have been used to describe the crisis developing in the North American church over the last twenty-five to thirty years. Our present crisis is underscored by the American Religious Identification Survey 2008. Not just one local congregation, but nearly every church is being swamped by the changes.

Volumes have already been written in analysis of the current situation and in critique of the church. I suggested a few books and workshops that I knew, trying to avoid the highly technical works. But the church leader with whom I was talking was overwhelmed by all the analysis. "Yes, I am sure that is true. But what do we do? When I look at what is happening and I hear all the criticism, I wonder if the church has a future at all. Do we deserve one?"

I emphasized that there are no simple answers and that those who offer simplistic solutions are either deceived or deceiving. There is no "church cookbook" for today (and I'm not sure there ever really was one). I tried to avoid an equally simplistic pietistic answer.

Still, the church leader pressed. "So, is the church dead? Do we just need to schedule a funeral and get over it? We are all so tired and frustrated."

I do not accept the sentiment of futility and despair about the future of the church. I believe that the church is alive and persists, not because of what we do, but because of what God has done and continues to do in the church.

The pain is real, however, as are the struggle and the longing. I wanted to help church leaders such as this one understand, but not be overwhelmed by the peculiar set of forces impacting the church today. But information was not enough. I wanted to encourage them with specific things that can be done, without implying that success is guaranteed or that human effort is sufficient. I wanted them to learn from what others are doing, not to copy them mechanically, but to use what others are doing as eyeglasses to look closely at their own context. I wanted them to avoid all the churchy labels that are out there and be a living church in their community, empowered and sustained by the living God.

Those of us who work with groups of churches and who pay attention to the things that are happening around us know that several forces are having a devastating effect on the church today. Both formal studies and personal observation identify at least eight key areas where the impact has been especially acute. These areas are biblical illiteracy, financial pressures, overwhelming diversity, shrinking numbers, declining leadership base, brokenness in and around us, narrowing inward focus, and unraveling of spiritual community. It is not hard to see how each of these is related to the others.

Living Church is a series from Judson Press intended to address each of these forces from a congregational perspective. While our authors are well informed biblically, theologically, and topically, these volumes are not intended to be an exercise in ecclesiastical academics. Our intent is to empower congregational leaders (both clergy and laity) to rise to the challenge before us.

Our goal is not merely to lament our state of crisis, but to identify creative and constructive strategies for our time and place so that we can move on to effective responses. Our time and place is the American church in the twenty-first century.

The first volume in this series, *Making Friends, Making Disciples,* by Dr. Lee Spitzer, addresses the issue of shrinking numbers by reminding us of the spiritual discipline of being and making friends, not with some ulterior motive, but because God has called us to relationship. The second volume, *Caring Pastors, Caring People,* by Dr. Marvin McMickle, confronts the growing brokenness within and around the church by challenging leaders who will reach out to provide pastoral care, both within the congregation and then in the community beyond.

The next volume, *Empowering Laity, Engaging Leaders,* by Susan Gillies and Ingrid Dvirnak, considers the declining leadership base in many churches today and asserts, "Church vitality depends on the involvement of both clergy and laity in meaningful ministry." Then *Learning Mission, Living Mission,* by Glynis LaBarre, argues that, at its core, mission is about demonstrating the reign of God. The church must travel with and learn from its surrounding community to become the missional church God has called us to be.

The fifth volume, *Vital Spirit, Vital Service: Spirituality That Works,* by Dr. Trinette McCray, challenges our media-saturated world by diving into the deep waters of Christian spirituality with a call to live "undivided and integrated lives where all we do is an expression of our faith."

In this latest volume, *Welcoming Community: Diversity That Works,* by Rev. Douglas Avilesbernal, we explore the challenge of exploding diversity (generationally, ethnically, and ideologically) in the North American church. A missionary kid with immigrant roots, Pastor Doug seeks to guide us on the path toward Christian diversity. Building a new "home" that reflects the rich diversity of God's creation is a theological imperative demonstrated in Jesus Christ and empowered by the Holy Spirit. This must come "from the depth of our Christian identity, born from profound relationship, that the call from Jesus draws its strength to effect changes within us." This is the way of true welcoming community—of *koinonia*. But because it demands change in ourselves and in our beloved churches, the process is deeply emotional. Pastor Doug rightly names this challenge—with its difficulties and its opportunities. Only through the guidance of the Spirit can we discern what must be turned loose and what must be embraced and cherished.

—Rev. Dr. J. Dwight Stinnett
Series Editor
Retired Executive Minister
American Baptist Churches, Great Rivers Region

Introduction:
Living in a New World

> Now there were staying in Jerusalem God-fearing Jews from every nation under heaven. When they heard this sound, a crowd came together in bewilderment, because each one heard their own language being spoken. (Acts 2:5-6, NIV)

Several years into my time at Calvary Baptist Church of Norristown, Pennsylvania, we decided to make some changes to our Christmas Eve service. As an example, traditionally the ending had been the lighting of the candles while we sing "Silent Night." That year, after "Silent Night," the lights came back on and the stirring notes of another carol began—Isaac Watts's beloved hymn, "Joy to the World."

When the lights came on and the unexpected music started, one of our new church attendees, a young man from Mexico, started walking toward the front of our worship space carrying something in his arms. People looked on in confusion as he made his way up the aisle. Those confused expressions changed as he arrived at the empty manger that we had placed right next to the large wreath with the Advent candles. He bent and placed his burden in it—a lifelike baby doll, obviously representing the newborn Jesus. It was wonderful to see people realize why the manger was so large that year and more importantly that the manger had been empty the entire time.

I did not get a chance to chat with many people that night. But, as the days passed and we moved into January, the comments started trickling in. The picture that began taking shape piece by piece, like stained glass, was of a profound and meaningful worship experience such as we had not had in a very long time. As with a stained-glass window, most of these pieces were different in color, shading, and size, but as they came together, it was clear that something amazing was there: all of us had experienced profound, life-giving worship. Interestingly, although each of us had experienced this in our own way, the changes to our traditional order of worship had been minimal.

What happened that changed our worship experience so much? We had a young man carry a doll that was to be baby Jesus for that evening. But it was not just what he was doing; it was how he was doing it. No one in that space could escape noticing how he carried the doll as gently as a new father would carry his newborn child. Joy, excitement, nervousness, and awe poured out of the young man's body. When he arrived at the front, he placed baby Jesus with utmost care in the manger. He then proceeded to tuck the baby in, taking his time, making sure that Jesus was comfortable, warm, and safe. After a good while, and only when he was fully satisfied that baby Jesus was going to be all right, did the young man return to his seat.

This young man was someone from the neighborhood who had come to our church building because of our English classes. The baby Jesus doll that he carried was one that he and I had bought at one of our local Mexican stores. Baby Jesus looked very much like he does in Roman Catholic paintings and churches. Purchasing the doll in our neighborhood was possible because there is a very popular tradition in Mexican households, either practicing Roman Catholic or cultural, to have a baby Jesus doll that is dressed up for Christmas Eve. The young man whom we chose to bring baby Jesus to the manger was a cultural Catholic.

For him, being given the honor of bringing Jesus to the manger was more than most of us, with our Protestant understanding of symbols, could comprehend.

These are the facts of the event. But there is more to the story.

On that Christmas Eve a young Catholic man far away from home, some older English and German descendants, and a brand-new Latino pastor worshiped in their own distinct way at the same time in the same place. Even better, on that Christmas Eve the arrival of Jesus created a home for several groups of people who up to that point knew very little about one another's worlds. What really happened was that the shock of the change took a step into the background, and the possibly bitter taste of change was sweetened by hope and visible love. That Christmas Eve grew all of our families in number and in depth. Such is the power of Christian multiculturalism to nurture change in a community of faith when it is rooted in love as we all have received it from God.

That Christmas Eve, our congregation witnessed a kind of Pentecost, where people of different cultures, languages, and backgrounds came together in a powerful moment of shared faith and worship. The Christmas Eve Pentecost that we experienced did not just happen. Nor can our life at the church after that day be superficially summarized with "And they lived happily ever after." Life is much too profound, relevant, and diverse for easy solutions and uninterrupted joy. But this wonderful experience does show that true Christian multiculturalism is a possibility for our churches. Diversity can and does work when we undergo the process as though it were life itself. In other words, Pentecost happened in the midst of a diversity that remained diverse through the experience.

Scripture tells us that the people who witnessed that history-making Pentecost in first-century Jerusalem heard their own languages; that is, there was something of home for them in that place at that time. On the day of Pentecost the Holy Spirit did not ask people to learn how to be Christian in the right way. They weren't even asked to learn the language of the land in order to be included in worship.

At the same time, a Pentecost experience is too deep and life-changing to be experienced well without preparation and work after that amazing event. Philip still needed to be whisked away in the spirit and dropped into the desert to affirm an Ethiopian who asked, "What's to prevent me from being baptized?" Jewish Peter still needed a thrice-repeated vision to prepare him for the Roman Cornelius. Paul and Barnabas still needed to go before the elders in Jerusalem to justify their ministry to the Gentile believers. In a similar way, Christian diversity does not happen without a complex emotional journey that must take place before or alongside any step-by-step program.

I have mentioned Christian diversity several times, so let me explain what I mean by this expression, as it is integral to our goal as followers of Christ. It seems to me that diversity as our culture understands it can take us only to tolerance, and that most of the available diversity training or strategy resources fall short of a Christ-driven life in diversity. Most resources seem to aim at enabling one person to approach another so as to no longer dislike but only to tolerate. There is nothing wrong with tolerance, especially when what is being addressed is prejudice against and ignorance of one another. However, to tolerate those different from ourselves means that we find a way to live with others by staying out of one another's way. By contrast, Christian diversity complicates this goal of toleration because Christ does not ask us only to learn to live alongside our neighbor. Accordingly, resources intended to help Christian communities welcome differences must be rooted in Christ's demand that we love one another as we love ourselves.

What I mean, then, by Christian diversity is a way of life that is far beyond toleration. It means life in community that welcomes and integrates differences as added riches that flow from God. On our way to that goal we will have to be willing to journey through Samaria and maybe even stop there to speak with a Samaritan (John 4:1-42).

But now let us consider why we seem to have such a difficult time achieving diversity. There are probably hundreds of books and programs with "easy steps" toward having a diverse church with explosive growth. I am sure that hundreds of consultants are ready to train us with catchy phrases, glossy brochures, videos, websites—the works. Of course, there is a place for solid methodology and perhaps even diversity consultants. But before they charge you big bucks "to position you for transition," ask yourselves if you are emotionally ready as individuals and as a congregation to leave home. It would not have been possible for us as a church to have had our Christmas Pentecost without a profound emotional journey toward the other as led by Jesus.

Make no mistake about it, the journey toward Christian diversity is a long, tough, winding road into our own version of Samaria that takes effort to traverse and is difficult to predict. What's worse, and great, is that at the end of the journey you will be in the same physical place from which you started. The difference will be that this time the journey to Christian diversity will not be a whole lot of work for nothing. Things certainly will be different, but instead of worrying you, these differences will be all right, or at the least you will be able to live in the different world. Christian diversity is indeed difficult because it is a world completely different from the one that most of us are used to.

The Hazards of Homogeneity

The status of the North American church with regard to diversity covers the full spectrum from complete isolation to a Kingdom-like embrace. For the purpose of this book, we will take as our starting place and working premise that the overwhelming majority of our churches on Sunday morning look very much like they looked in the 1950s. Homogeneity is the norm even when a church is ethnically diverse. There is a denomination (they would be loath to be called such) that is ethnically diverse but very much like the 1950s in homogeneous socioeconomic, educational, and therefore cultural terms. Some may say that megachurches are the exception, but the emotional walls of segregation are kept there as well. So, for the purpose of this book, our beginning is that diversity is elusive, and most of us worship with those most like us. That is a problem.

Meanwhile, the world outside our churches does not look at all like the 1950s. Hardly anything about the overt homogeneity and appearance of conformity from that time is left. Sunday mornings are no longer about church. People feel no guilt about not being in church on Sunday morning, even if their only reason is that they want to sleep in. The world outside our church walls has changed dramatically, but we have changed little inside the church. This reality alienates us even more, thus compounding the difficulties of reaching out to the other.

There is such a distance between us and our relevance to those outside church that even a cursory look at where we are clearly lets us know we are in a completely different world physically and emotionally. We are now in an entirely new place that is as foreign to many of us as we are to those outside our walls. The new place where we find ourselves is not pleasant, nor is it one where hope is visible. In many ways, despair seems to be the only feasible response to the challenges facing us as the local congregation. Of course, we always have choices in life. Indeed, there are few times in life and leadership where one is truly trapped.

That said, it does seem that the traditional church (in the positive sense of that phrase) now finds itself in a perceived corner with only one or two ways out, each of which proceeds through a strange and distrusted land, a modern kind of Samaria. We feel trapped and at the mercy of a new world that we cannot understand. That world seems to tell us that the price of escape into life again is leaving behind who we are—compromising our time-honored traditions and even our essential convictions about faith.

So, is there a way for the church to live into the present while honoring tradition and keeping the past alive? Is it possible for the pipe organ and the worship band to exist in the same church and be valued equally? Can youth who love electronic media come together with the elders who love the hymnal and grow spiritually and in numbers together? These are some of the questions that this book seeks to explore. In order for this journey of exploration to bear fruit, we need to do an honest self-assessment as individuals and as a local church. We should also look to assess where we think the world that we are trying to reach is, which probably means that we bring in fresh eyes to explain it to us.

The first several chapters of this book will be a guided journey into self-assessment. We need to know where we think our congregation is emotionally and where it wants to go. That journey will also take us to a vantage point from which we will look out at our immediate world and see how consequential we are to our neighbors.

Our exploration will take us around our world to gain distance from ourselves and see some things more clearly. We are in a period of upheaval in which the traditional mores of faith have been uprooted and the resulting instability has left the faithful gasping for air and uncertain of what it means to be church in our current societal context. In the midst of this storm of uncertainty, it is natural to grasp at any bit of certainty perceived. Some have chosen to circle the wagons and resist, even if it means the death of the church. Others have searched for the new place in church through experimental ways by calling themselves "church 2.0"[1] and many other catchy names.

When we add the postmodern mindset—that there are many versions of truth—to this mix, we end up with a landscape of fiefdoms all seeking to be the next Holy Roman Empire. The old families (mainline churches) seem incapable of moving beyond living off their names and traditions, so they are constantly overrun by the newer, more energetic upstarts who are strange and nearly blasphemous to them. The storied families that know safety in their institutions retreat to their historic castles, shut the doors, and shout to all those outside to come into the fortress to weather the storm. Meanwhile, the newer churches (many with big-name pastors) run around in apparent freedom trying out various places, styles of worship, and theology.

In the middle of this new era of charismatic leaders versus storied denominations, we find local congregations simply trying to survive. Should they run to the fortress, close the doors, and shout dire warnings from the safety of the institution (even though these fortresses seem more like prisons to those outside?) Or should they join the interlopers in exploring and testing as they search for a home that fulfills those deeply held longings that the paradigm shift in the church has left exposed and uncared for?

The Challenges of Change

When we have explored who we are and the world around us, we will also look into the consequences of leading change in times of crisis. Those of us in leadership during this monumental shift are also trapped in a maze of tough choices. Push too much, and the church that we are leading could be lost; push too little, and the church could die.

If we push too much too soon, we could leave the older congregants feeling like we are asking them to cheat on a past that they love and still live with. The problem is deeper still because it is not only a matter of disenfranchising older people living in the past. Leaving behind the past behind and making a clean break may appeal to a new generation of leaders, and on the whole it is easier to carry out. However, in doing so we lose a wealth of good and needed practices and traditions and a historic connection with the greater family of God.

I recently read an article that stated, "Today if young people aren't happy with a system, they'll either find a better one or create their own."[2] The article ostensibly was written to help churches in denominational relationships understand where all the millennials have gone. I continue to be terribly saddened by that sentence because I find it wrong in just about any way I think about it. On the one hand, it assumes that millennials don't know about relationships enough to fight for any of them. On the other hand, it does speak prophetically to church systems incapable of adjusting to change. If we are unable to let the younger generations know that we are listening by hearing them and doing something, they will indeed leave and create their own faith communities.

In any case, a wedge is being driven into the people of God. The congregations that seem to suffer most are the churches with the longest history. In these communities, we find an appreciation for the traditions of the space that they occupy—something rare in our culture. Perhaps some do go overboard with their love, but this is partly due to the pushback from society in general. For many in these traditional churches there is a sense of importance regarding events and people who have inhabited the particular church. There are many reasons for this appreciation, the majority of which are often rooted in the fact that there are still people in these churches who remember the good things that happened or knew those who led the church to good things.

Another aspect of this thinking is that there are still visual cues of the "good" that once inhabited these churches. Many of these places still have the great stone buildings, with their intricate and beautiful architecture safely resting on sound masonry not often seen anymore. Such great stone edifices are gorgeously adorned with awe-inspiring stained glass that warms the look of the stone building on the outside and lets in light that illuminates images of the glory of God to the increasingly fewer worshipers inside. As if such beauty weren't enough, there is also the gorgeous design of the worship space often ably enhanced by the sound and look of the pipe organ. All of it put together points to a greatness that, when properly explained and received, embodies the awesomeness and otherness of God.

Such beauty alone is good enough, for many to want to preserve it and fight for its preservation. When we add the fact that many of these people also know the human beauty of Christian community in that place, it becomes easier to see why many of us are trapped in a particular church as it is. A member of the congregation who remembers being taken to church by the person after whom the fellowship hall is named is indeed trapped by that place, and gladly so!

So, to come in and tell these lifelong members that most, if not all, of what they hold dear and precious about their church is old-fashioned and needs to go is a recipe for conflict that kills churches. To suddenly shift them into a "new church world" is tantamount to asking them to cheat on their past. It is asking people to discard a very real "something" that they have cherished in happy times and that has sustained them in difficult times. In other words, a big part of why many of these churches are failing is the faith and everlasting love of its members. These faithful people love deeply and will remain loyal past their dying breath. Do not ask them to cheat on their past by becoming something they are not.

Some time ago my congregation at Calvary Baptist of Norristown needed to find a new music minister. We decided to make use of all that technology had to offer and place our information in online boards rather than in printed outlets. We were able to attract a good number of candidates even though our salary was not a very high one. We were looking for someone comfortable with a traditional service and able to play a pipe organ who could also lead a contemporary service on the piano. As we began receiving applications, we ran into the specialization that permeates our world now. We found organists who did not care for contemporary music. We found contemporary worship leaders who were sometimes surprised that we still had and used an organ in church. (One person said to me, "Of course I don't play the organ. That is a dying art, and no successful church I know of is looking to maintain a traditional service.")

Other worship leaders sounded like band leaders looking for a gig: How big is your worship band, and what's the instrumentation? How many channels does your sound board have, and how experienced is your sound technician? Very few of them showed any interest in the mission of the church unless it included a marketable growth plan.

The new church movement seems to be asking those who have sustained our faith life for the last century to discard all that they love for the sake of an untested way of doing church that is more a show than a worship service. Our long-term and faithful churches are being asked to cheat on their past while they're still living with it. How can the church live into a new world while embracing new paradigms as well as remaining deeply rooted in a gospel that it has come to know only through the traditions, now seemingly obsolete, that it inherited from those who came before?

Throughout this book I will discuss some ways we take the journey toward Christian diversity in a way that loves all and seeks to keep all. *Christ*ian diversity is indiscriminate in giving love, fully embracing of difference, and eager to become family with the other. At the center of this endeavor is the fundamental fact that the emotional process will determine the outcome of the journey. In fact, the majority of this book focuses on the emotional journey prior to reaching out to embrace diversity. As I mentioned before, there are plenty of how-to methods for growing a multicultural church. All of them come with success stories that are guaranteed to excite you or make you jealous enough to want to try them. But few if any of them also tell you about the heavy emotional toll that these journeys demand from the congregation and its leaders.

The result of not preparing emotionally for the journey to Samaria is that churches end in a perennial New Year's resolution cycle. The list of things that we *could* do is endless and appealing, so we keep starting things and thinking that this time it will work. Engaging in an intentional and profound emotional process as individuals and as a church can be just what we need in order to stop the endless cycle and begin a journey to actual change and an embracing of all of God's children, especially the Samaritans.

Notes

1. See Randy Frizee, *The Connecting Church 2.0: Beyond Small Groups to Authentic Community* (Grand Rapids: Zonderman, 2013).

2. Shayne Raynor, "While You Were Wondering Where All the Millennials Went . . . ," MinistryMatters, January 26, 2015, http://www.ministrymatters.com/all/entry/5731/while-you-were-wondering-where-the-millennials-went?

Epigraph

Now when Jesus learned that the Pharisees had heard, "Jesus is making and baptizing more disciples than John"—although it was not Jesus himself but his disciples who baptized—he left Judea and started back to Galilee. But he had to go through Samaria. So he came to a Samaritan city called Sychar, near the plot of ground that Jacob had given to his son Joseph. Jacob's well was there, and Jesus, tired out by his journey, was sitting by the well. It was about noon.

A Samaritan woman came to draw water, and Jesus said to her, "Give me a drink." (His disciples had gone to the city to buy food.) The Samaritan woman said to him, "How is it that you, a Jew, ask a drink of me, a woman of Samaria?" (Jews do not share things in common with Samaritans.) Jesus answered her, "If you knew the gift of God, and who it is that is saying to you, 'Give me a drink,' you would have asked him, and he would have given you living water." The woman said to him, "Sir, you have no bucket, and the well is deep. Where do you get that living water? Are you greater than our ancestor Jacob, who gave us the well, and with his sons and his flocks drank from it?" Jesus said to her, "Everyone who drinks of this water will be thirsty again, but those who drink of the water that I will give them will never be thirsty. The water that I will give will become in them a spring of water gushing up to eternal life." The woman said to him, "Sir, give me this water, so that I may never be thirsty or have to keep coming here to draw water."

Jesus said to her, "Go, call your husband, and come back." The woman answered him, "I have no husband." Jesus said to her, "You are right in saying, 'I have no husband'; for you have had five husbands, and the one you have now is not your husband. What you have said is true!" The woman said to him, "Sir, I see that you are a prophet. Our ancestors worshiped on this mountain, but you say that the place where people must worship is in Jerusalem." Jesus said to her, "Woman, believe me, the hour is coming when you will worship the Father neither on this mountain nor in Jerusalem. You worship what you do not know; we worship what we know, for salvation is from the Jews. But the hour is coming, and is now here, when the true worshipers will worship the Father in spirit and truth, for the Father seeks such as these to worship him. God is spirit, and those who worship him must worship in spirit and truth." The woman said to him, "I know that Messiah is coming" (who is called Christ). "When he comes, he will proclaim all things to us." Jesus said to her, "I am he, the one who is speaking to you." (John 4:1-25, NRSV)

CHAPTER 1

Identifying New Realities

Go therefore and make disciples of all nations, baptizing them in the name of the Father and of the Son
and of the Holy Spirit. (Matthew 28:19, NRSV)

Many challenges face local congregations, those with storied pasts
as well as those that may be past their prime or just encountering
obstacles in our new and cruel world. As a result, some say that the
traditional churches should close in favor of the cool, hip, happening, 2.0, next church. Meanwhile, in too many local churches there
are faithful people frantically looking for ways to get Jesus to come
over to their house to help their ill churches, as we see the faithful
do in the Gospels (e.g., Mark 5:21-24; Luke 7:1-8). There are more
reasons than this book can cover to explain our long and effective
journey toward the fringes of society and loss of influence. But first
we should look back to shed some light on a few of the reasons
why we are where we are.

Recalling Our History

Jesus' call in Matthew 28 has been a rallying cry for churches for
centuries. We in the United States have gladly taken the mantle
these past several centuries. Jonathan Edwards heard that call and
set to work on what would be one of our great revivals. The Azusa

Street Mission, the origin of our modern pentecostal movement, was founded on the principle of reaching out to all people, regardless of race. Of course, that fact didn't thrill some people. As far back as the beginning of the twentieth century, while some churches were being led by God's call in Matthew 28 to welcome all in their midst, the establishment looked on with worry and sometimes even horror. The renowned preacher Charles Parham said of the Azusa revival, "Men and women, white and blacks, knelt together or fell across one another; a white woman, perhaps of wealth and culture, could be seen thrown back in the arms of a big 'buck nigger,' and held tightly thus as she shivered and shook in freak imitation of Pentecost. Horrible, awful shame."[1]

In the past two centuries, the zeal for reaching out was fueled in great part by being a society in which being Christian was taken for granted.[2] The church was an integral part of society; belief in God and respect for the institution of the church were as American as apple pie. People knew that they were expected to go to church. Therefore, our churches were full, and the energy was palpable—all we needed to do was open the doors. The result was decades of growth in which our buildings and programs kept pace with that progress. Worship was relevant to life, and church activities were creative responses to the needs in our neighborhoods. In generations past, Calvary Baptist Church of Norristown held evenings of family square dancing at a time when there were plenty of young families familiar with square dancing. These events were always well attended.

Those times were also when Christian leaders were trusted and respected in matters of faith and morality; the pastor was consulted on important matters in towns all around our country. During these heady times Billy Graham, who for decades served as the country's de facto national pastor, could visit with the president of the United States and then speak to a full press corps eager for a word from the wise man of God. Christianity was so embedded in society that adding the phrase "under God" to the pledge of allegiance during the 1950s did not create noticeable protest.[3] We also enjoyed a long history of Sunday being reserved for church activities alone by religious and civic law.[4] Only a handful of states still enforce so-called blue laws that restrict certain activities (such as selling cars or alcohol) on Sundays.

In many ways the 1950s were the height of the cultural church's remarkable trajectory of influence over the previous two centuries. From the 1800s to just about the 1960s the Christian church in the United States experienced nearly uninterrupted success in earthly and spiritual terms. Because our churches were full, our major concerns revolved around building expansions. Our buildings were majestic examples of our love and awe of God, as well as our giving. At a deeper level, our houses of worship were well thought-out representations of the eternal in tangible forms. Yet, as with much of our faith then and now, they also represented the flawed humanity in each of us as each church sought to outdo the other faithful's church building "for the glory of God."

Inspired by the call in Matthew's Gospel and being well funded by dutiful and generous members, we developed a missionary system that would eventually reach the majority of our world. By the early 1950s we had nearly conquered our country and the world. Armed with continued success and great resources, we gradually came to believe that we knew how to "do" church in the best way. As we lived out the decade, our churches remained full and our coffers were replenished steadily. We lived in a world full of certainties in which the church had the answers and the government was trusted.

Then, in the early 1960s something changed. The generations coming of age in that decade began to question all of the social moorings, including the church. Business also started to trespass on God time as more and more business owners began to challenge or disregard blue laws. All of this turmoil showed most evidently in young people as they began to leave church, grow their hair long, and explore their freedom of choice in rebellious and unheard-of ways. As if these changes were not enough to shake the church, there came a massive shift in our everyday lives as a result of the civil rights movement and subsequent federal legislation. Suddenly, the stable and certain world that Christians in the United States had enjoyed for decades was violently shaken to its core. Truths that had been taken for granted were not only challenged openly but also even ignored. By the middle of the 1960s it was clear that the world was changing, and from the perspective of many churches, these changes were for the worse.

Many of our churches chose to fight these changes and try to regain lost ground. When it became clear that an alarming attrition rate was threatening all of our congregations, we tried to get "them" back with the worship and fellowship activities that were meaningful to us in the old days, but to no avail. The world had moved on without us. We no longer knew our neighborhood, much less the world. So, our activities and ministries failed to connect with people who by then were little more than distant acquaintances. We were too busy doing our best to preserve what the previous one hundred years had shown us to be correct to notice our slide toward the fringe of society. As a result, we drifted into a long and increasingly deeper isolation where preservation became more important that exploration.

Nonetheless, sustained by our inherited funds and the faithful giving of those who remained, we closed in and grew comfortable. We drifted from being living members of our communities into insular havens from a terrible world. We held firm and fought the devil, new life, and people out of our churches.

Seeing Ourselves as Others See Us

Some time ago I was asked to officiate the funeral of someone who for decades had not been at the church I was pastoring. As I arrived at the funeral home, I looked for the funeral director, because I had only spoken with members of the family on the phone. While waiting, I realized that I was standing close enough to hear a conversation between a grandson of the deceased and a family friend. After some time the conversation turned to who was going to officiate the funeral.

> **Grandson:** Well, he used to go to Calvary. I remember Grandpa used to take us there when we were little, and we loved just running around that building once the big Sunday school class was over. Man! That was a great church with lots of people [*said in a sad tone*].
> **Family friend:** So, is the pastor from there coming?
> **Grandson:** I doubt it. I don't even think the church is still open. The building is still there, but I never see anybody when I drive by. Plus, it was going downhill thirty years ago when Grandpa left.

The members of our church would have been devastated to hear anyone speak that way of what they knew to be still a vibrant church. The interesting thing about this story is that both perspectives were right and wrong at the same time. The church was not closed in the way the man's grandson thought, but the church was not alive in the way the remaining church members thought. Therein lies one of the biggest current challenges to our local congregations. We are no longer who we were, but many of us refuse to acknowledge that to ourselves. So, we plan and expect results partly based on the image that we have of our church that no longer exists in the current world. Another way of putting it is to say that we are so close to the church we love that we cannot or will not see or understand how it is no longer at the center of life in our town and society in general.

Thinking of our congregation in exaggerated terms does not make us strange or signal that there is something wrong with us. In fact, thinking of our local church in such terms means that we are normal and are living a common perception problem that permeates our world and even helps us at times to make sense of our environment. This misleading perception of the self and our world has come to be known as *confabulation*. We think we know when we are lying to ourselves, but in truth, "you are often ignorant of your motivations and create fictional narratives to explain your decisions, emotions, and history without realizing it."[5] So it is then that one person can think of a church as being closed while those who attend think of it as the wonderful pillar of the town that they have always known. I suspect that this experience could be familiar around our country. There are wonderful churches with great, long histories of faithful following of Christ, but some neighbors in their communities have wondered if the building is still even open.

The North American church has an amazing story of blessed success that spans centuries. The local congregation has always been the driving force in the life of the church in the United States. Yet, as we face a brave new world, people may have started to believe that the local congregation's time has passed. As we look for a solution to this dilemma, we will be tempted to look in various places, and the diversity of new church styles points to that search. However, as we search, we must remember that although our past can be a burden if misused, experience well used is worth much more than any of the new trends in getting people into church.

The local congregation has been instrumental in bringing the love of God to the people of God. By necessity, the local congregation must be local, in town and with its neighbors. The world has changed, but our response need not be to become more like the world, including its view of success. Rather, becoming active and contributing neighbors will lead us to learn more about those around us. The resulting closeness will take us the rest of the way toward translating God's relevance to our current world. We have always been locally sourced, and our relevance is dependent on us remaining so.

Understanding a Multicultural World

Much has changed during the church's more recent cultural isolation in the United States, but few things have changed as much as the way diversity is lived. The blurring of long-established racial and social lines has shaken the church profoundly. As a result, the movement toward a society that is much more tolerant and embracing of multiculturalism has been tremendously difficult for congregations. The main reason is that many of us do not know how to navigate life without our guiding social or racial parameters. In the past, there were rules to follow, and we all were expected to adhere to them. Some rules were as simple as knowing that a Baptist would not date a Lutheran, much less a Catholic, and even less thinkable, a Jew. (It was highly unlikely that a Baptist would even know a Muslim, Buddhist, or Hindu.) Back then, controversial "mixed" marriages were between people of, say, Irish versus Italian descent. More incontrovertibly, "everyone knew" that you don't mix races voluntarily. People of color, whether black, Hispanic, Native American, or Asian, were "off limits" to anyone of Anglo-European ancestry. What do we do now that all the rules that have "kept the peace" at church seem to be gone?

In thinking about what to do in this new brave world where all the norms and rules that helped us know our place have fallen by the wayside, we are once again brought back to looking at ourselves as objectively as possible. For example, since the civil rights movement broke down many public walls, many of us are tempted to think that our churches and society are in a world that is past those struggles. Yet we know that the private walls have proven much more resistant. Alongside these private walls, local churches have been some of the most efficient and strong supporting load-bearing walls for maintaining segregation, so much so that in spite of how blurred ethnic lines may be outside our walls, most of us still worship with those who are most like us. It has proven difficult for many churches to make the transition into our new, diverse reality.

With this new reality has come the fact that the days when everyone kept to the places where they "belonged" and kept company with the people they "should" are long gone, especially in many of the places where our churches are located. Of course, there are enclaves where separation is the norm, and probably there will always be such places. Although the days when homogeneous congregations could be enforced as the norm are gone, our history and the experience of God's people, the Israelites, show us a way forward.

Notes

1. Charles F. Parham, "Free Love," *Apostolic Faith* 1, no. 10 (December 1912): 4–5. *Apostolic Faith* was located in Baxter Springs, Arkansas.

2. According to Gallup polling, 91 percent of people asked about their religious affiliation identified themselves as Christians in the late 1940s and into the 1950s. See Frank Newport, "Questions and Answers about Americans' Religion," December 24, 2007, http://www.gallup.com/poll/103459/Questions-Answers-About-Americans-Religion.aspx.

3. John Baer, *The Pledge of Allegiance: A Revised History and Analysis* (Annapolis, MD: Free State Press, 2007).

4. Peter Wallenstein, *Blue Laws and Black Codes: Conflicts, Courts, and Change in Twentieth-Century Virginia* (Charlottesville: University of Virginia Press, 2004).

5. David McRaney, *You Are Not So Smart: Why You Have Too Many Friends on Facebook, Why Your Memory Is Mostly Fiction, and 46 Other Ways You're Deluding Yourself* (New York: Gotham Books, 2011), 14.

CHAPTER 2

Encountering New Realities

> Surely the LORD your God has blessed you in all your
> undertakings; he knows your going through this
> great wilderness. (Deuteronomy 2:7, NRSV)

When assessing where its congregation is in the face of the new
realities of the world in which we live, a church may encounter two
factors that make it long for the past: loss of clout and shift in
resources. In our journey toward Christian diversity it is important
to recognize aspects of the journey that will make longing for the
past very tempting. Just as the people of God found themselves in
a difficult new world during the exodus, so will a church moving
toward a community of Christian diversity. However, in that
process, we can come to understand that even though we feel that
we're in a wilderness, God will guide us through it, just as the Lord
did with the ancient Israelites.

Obstacles to Building Community

Loss of Clout

During the "good old days" our churches were full of rules and
behavioral expectations that enforced conformity in those attending. The most obvious rule was the dress codes. Everyone knew that
you had to dress a certain way to go to church. Our connection with

society was such that it also became the rule outside of church. The dress code often included length of hair for women and men, as well as facial hair (or absence of it) for men. Somewhere in the midst of our incredible success we came to believe that everything had be regulated, and that those who did not adhere to our church rules could not be Christians with us.

Enforcing our Christianity on those who came to church was easy when the majority of society accepted the rules and contributed by either enforcing them or adhering to them. But now we have people coming to church who don't know that those rules exist. We often have a group of "insiders" trying to enforce something on another group, "outsiders" who do not know the rules that they are supposed to be following. The result often is frustration on both sides that keeps community from building.

During the Spanish conquest, every time conquistadors came to the land of an established group, they had to inform the people and their rightful, God-ordained king that their land had been given to the Spanish monarchs by the pope. The Spaniards informed the new people by reading a document given to them by their own kings. This document was called *el requerimiento* ("the requirement") and was to be read by the clergy so that those hearing it knew that it had the force of the church and thus of God. The document always was read in Spanish and, more often than not, beyond earshot of the natives because the cleric who was reading feared for his life. However, once the document was read, the land was deemed officially Spain's, and thus the conquistadors could move in and force the locals into service as vassals of the Spanish king. Any resistance would then be considered treason, because these locals were now under the care of the crown. Thus the Spanish were free to enslave or kill the traitors without fear of punishment from law or God. The *requerimiento* helped the Spaniards, as it made room for them (in their understanding of faith) to enslave people.

Every time I have read about how the *requerimiento* was used, I have wondered how the Spanish did not see the irony of the practice. The truth is that they probably did, but it allowed them to justify their purely earthly actions. In a similar way, the kingdoms that we created came to be more after our own image than God's.

We think of ourselves as more advanced than the people of those times. Yet, during the early 1960s, when young men started to grow their hair and beards long, when women wanted to choose for themselves and be taken seriously, and when all started to question the things that they had been told to follow "just because," faithful church leaders and members read *requerimientos* to them too. Our clergy decided to stand under gorgeous stained-glass windows or beautiful oil paintings of a person looking exactly like these young people and tell them to shave their beards, cut their hair, get rid of that loose, sloppy clothing, and wear suits like a good follower of Christ would.

So it was then that beginning in the 1960s or so, by way of our intransigence, the Christian church found itself losing cultural clout. We did not realize at that time how the ground was eroding under our feet. So we kept going, doing, and being all we knew while wondering why there were fewer and fewer people in church. In response, we found reasons based in our prejudices: if only these people would dress decently, shave, cut their hair, and be here on Sunday mornings, this whole thing would be fixed. If these hippies were not so lazy, our churches would be full again!

In fact, we are still giving *requerimientos* to people when they come through our doors. Bible study must be on Wednesday evening either at church or someone's house, and we require people to join a committee in order to allow them to help. We expect antiestablishment youth to know our church language; we want them to know the importance of our church institutions like we do, to dress a certain way, and to share the gospel in the right way instead of with their smartphones or social media. I'm sure that you can think of other contemporary *requerimientos.*

We all know that change isn't easy, especially changing a model that has been so successful for so long. We were incredibly effective for more than one hundred years. The problem is that we failed to notice that although the gospel has not changed, the way in which the world understands and hears it has. We no longer have the clout to enforce our understanding of church on all. So, we are ill-equipped to deal with a world that has moved on without us.

We have been in the wilderness for a while. We are unwilling to see or are unsure about the reasons that brought us where we are. In order for us to begin finding our way in this wilderness, there are tough steps to take. The changes in our world may require a trip from us to Jesus that is similar to the way he took his disciples to Samaria. We need to follow Jesus into places we do not want to go because of the people who are there. Like Nicodemus (John 3:1-21), we in the establishment need to seek out the outsider Jesus and listen to him tell us that we need to be born again. Perhaps those who need Jesus most are those of us inside the churches every Sunday.

A Shift in Resources

One of the most difficult things for congregations today to accept is that the world outside our walls no longer needs us as much as we need one another. Traditionally in the United States, the church has always done charity work for the neediest. When we have encountered those outside our walls, we have seen them as people in need. Therefore, the church's relationship with the needy has always been an unequal relationship with one side thinking that it has the lion's share of the resources. Additionally, our experience with the majority of the needy has been that often they have been the most recently arrived immigrants, particularly in urban environments. Yet, as our memberships have dwindled but our budgets have grown, our needs increased to the point where many of our congregations are no longer the stable church helping the less fortunate.

The result of the loss of people, resources, and clout has moved some churches from helping the needy to being the needy. As a result, churches find themselves having to engage with the world around them on more equal terms. Essentially, leaders in local churches need to ask those who know themselves as the "haves" to join the "have-nots" in a common search for how to be Christ's church with few resources of various kinds.

As we trace this trajectory, the magnitude of the challenge at hand becomes clearer. The exterior problems, such as a society that sees the church with suspicion or newer generations of people who dislike institutions, are making outreach difficult and frustrating. On the inside of our churches we also have both shrinking resources and leaders who are at a loss as to how to be relevant to the world around them. The difficulties are compounded by the fact that all of these matters are tremendously influenced by an emotional process that many are not even aware of and most are unwilling to explore.

One useful tool for leaders to measure this difficulty is to observe how the congregation deals with its resources when it comes to using them for ministry within. What leaders should look for is what the congregation expects from those to whom their ministry intended to help. You see, some churches have been blessed so much throughout their history that they have grown accustomed to engaging in relationship with the other through the giving of resources. Therefore, as responsible funders, we have grown to expect certain levels of deference from those whom we are helping. The questions to ask then are as follows: How does a congregation decide what resources and services a ministry recipient requires? How much input is the church willing to take from those it is helping? Do we solicit their own self-assessment of need, or do we make decisions based on our own judgments and opinions?

The responses to these questions may be helpful in coming to see the reason for many of the difficulties inherent in being forced to move to a more equal engagement with the world at large. Churches are no longer at the center of our communities, nor do we have the same type of means to help (and control) as we once did. As one missionary child friend of mine who wishes to remain anonymous observes:

> I often spent time with mission teams who would come to help their sisters and brothers in Latin America. As I grew I began to notice how much the arrival of these missions groups asked from their hosts. I also noticed how often they would become frustrated when things did not go the way they thought things should go. As I grew older I was increasingly asked to translate for these groups at functions, worksites, and other places. It was during many of those interactions that I realized more fully how difficult these trips were for a good group of people from both sides. On the Anglo side I often witnessed the usual struggles with time schedules and all the "wasted" time asking about family and friends when there were things to do, and many more. What surprised me was how deeply felt and broad these difficulties were. Many things were simply "wrong," and there was little room to see the cultural differences at the root of those things.
>
> These difficulties would go from the small things, like a frustrated American becoming angry because all the measurements in the materials were in the metric system and therefore not in the "right" sizes, to

watching my dad having to hear a "leader" berate him because he was not capable of making sure the local "helpers" would keep to a schedule. So, things would start late, services at church would go longer than expected, and as a result work suffered. Then on the local side I watched prejudices grow and be fed to the point where "gringos" were bossy, didn't care much for your opinion, and treated you as though you didn't know much.

There were many exceptions, as there continue to be. However, such stories illustrate part of our current struggles to move into a more diverse congregational understanding of church. It is difficult to move to equality when one has always been in charge. It is difficult to share a journey with those who are no longer the needy but are our equals in need.

Like the ancient Israelites, we are wandering in the wilderness. Being in the wilderness demands a massive change in the way we approach church. We need to find a way to shift from being church as we have always known into something that keeps its core while it adjusts to a new world. We need to come to the full realization that in order to continue being church as we have been in past generations, we would need the clout to enforce our church's Christianity on others. But we no longer have the clout. Therefore, we need to approach church as a follower of Christ, not necessarily as the saints charged with leading people to Christ.

Navigating the Wilderness

So far this chapter has been gloomy and perhaps even painful or offensive to read. Such negativity does raise the question "Is it really that bad?" The answer to that question depends on your particular situation. I suspect that your answer of how bad it is for your local church will fall somewhere on a fairly broad spectrum. But for the sake of our journey here, let us assume that your situation is as bad as or worse than described so far.

If things are very bad, what does it mean for your congregation?

You may be surprised how little it matters how bad things are for the purpose of this journey. What does matter is that we find a way to take inventory of where we are so that we gain perspective and with it more clarity. Far from being a guilt trip, an honest self-assessment is a fact-finding detour more akin to the beginning of a building project. We know that we don't have all the tools we need. Which tools do we think we're missing? Do we really need those tools? Can we use another tool that we already have to get us through that step? We need to look at where we are lacking as objectively as we can so that it moves from a heavy emotional load that we do not know how to handle to a difficulty that is just another part of our journey.

Why is it so important to find a beginning? We cannot plan a solution for a problem if we do not clearly know what the problem is. Interestingly enough, seeing how bad things are is not enough to find the beginning that we need. However, understanding more about how we arrived at this particular state of decline does point us in the right direction. But exploring how we feel about how bad these things are is what will take us to the beginning that we are searching for. All that I have discussed to this point could be kept at an intellectual, how-to level, and if we do so, we can even devise wonderful-looking plans that account for a great deal of the symptoms of our problems. But if we do not dig into how we feel about our problems, we will have a difficult time making the changes necessary to live into the transformation that this journey could birth. Any church renewal plan—especially one that requires crossing traditional social boundaries of culture and race or ethnicity—must account for the emotional process of the congregation.

Assessing the Emotional Process

A church in Pennsylvania was undergoing a church renewal self-assessment process. One of the exercises in the process was to ask the leaders of the church to plan what would be done as part of the closing of their church. Participants were given a certain amount of time to discuss the matter, after which they would return to the meeting and share their plans for closing. When the leaders came back, the mood was somber, and some people showed anger. When the instructor asked the first church member to discuss her plan, she said that she did not have one. When the instructor pressed her for an answer, she replied that she could not get herself even to consider the possibility of her church closing. Further, since this was supposed to be a church growth plan, she saw no need to look into the bad, "which we all already know," she said as she looked around.

All of us are good at hiding those things that need the most change within us, especially from ourselves. If we do not look into and process the emotional baggage of our congregation, we will continue to make plans that will be sabotaged by our feelings of anxiety, frustration, pain, fear of loss, and others. Sweeping these feelings under the rug is the reason why church members still struggling at the church can sabotage themselves and their community by looking for blame, responding from anger, or refusing to listen. One example of unexplored emotional response is talking about people who do not come to church in this way: "We bend over backwards for these people, and they just don't come!" If we do not explore our emotional baggage, that baggage will be the one that responds to trouble instead of us. In the case of the those who give the "we bend over backwards" response, we can see that anger has blinded them so much that there is no desire to look for a way to change what has been done, and so instead what comes out is misguided blame. We try what we know, which is not relevant to the world around us, yet expect the results that came when it was relevant. So, "It's their fault—people who do not come or have left the church—that we're not growing!"

Facing how we have contributed to the difficulty of our situation is a sobering experience. It is difficult to revisit our self-image by way of a journey of self-discovery. In that journey we may find that we, as the church, do not matter to our current society in the way we think we do. But learning more about how it is that we are seen by others can go a long way in helping us to create more appropriate responses. For if we do not know where we are and how we are seen, we may be creating responses to issues that do not exist.

For example, we all know that church is a good place to be, and Jesus is the way, and all the other ways of describing church that we learned in Sunday school. But the world around us sees us in a way different from what we would want. In many cases we, as the church, do not matter because other people do not know why we should matter. So, a ministry based on the assumption that the people we are trying to reach know that the church in general (and our congregation in particular) is a good place to be could be ineffective. Thus, the ministry's lack of effectiveness is not an indictment on how good the church can be. Rather, the lack of effectiveness has more to do with the fact that some ministries are answers based on nonexistent premises.

If we do not look at ourselves with honesty, we will remain lost in the wilderness. We will not able to find a clear destination, much less a way to explain to those around us who we are in an effective way. Yet, in the midst of this continued darkness the wonderful news about these problems is that we are not where we are because we are bad. We have had a hand in our decline, yes, but we also have the power to change course. To be sure, we have been thrown into the wilderness where those around us are not like we are, so it is difficult to communicate with them. But our potential to be an important part of our community remains and can be realized if we journey on to rediscover what it means to be followers of Christ where and when we live.

Resisting Consumerism

Furthering the community church's sense of loss is the explosion of megachurches. These places offer the complete package for the whole family. There are megachurches with a children's church budget bigger than the entire budget of many local congregations. These congregations no longer meet in historic church buildings; instead, they meet in warehouses, arenas, or stadiums that are designed more as a concert venue than a sanctuary as the church has known it for centuries. How could small local congregations even consider competing with them for new members? Many of our local congregations are closer to the needy side of the wealth spectrum, so to spend thousands of dollars on marketing alone for the children's summer camp is beyond consideration. How can the traditional local church survive in this merciless new world?

Before we despair, we should revisit the premise of competing with the megachurch. To begin with, there really is no competition. As the African saying goes, "Why should an ant try to choke an elephant?" Perhaps the question then should instead be, "Why does a small congregation feel the need to compete at all?"

One important aspect of this need to compete is imperceptibly fed by our consumerist society. All our lives we have learned from various outlets that the solution to our problems, worries, and anxieties is found in purchasing something. By now, consumerism is so ingrained in our psyche that we may not realize the extent to which this model affects us. It follows then that many small churches quite literally buy into the newest church growth model that created the five-thousand-member church from only twenty somewhere in the Midwest. Of course, a corollary to the need to grow through purchasing is that as we get smaller, our purchasing power is reduced and our sense of helplessness or entrapment by our own situation increases. The result could be a vicious cycle in which a church that wishes to grow finds itself looking to purchase its way out of the crisis with dwindling resources and frustrated givers.

Closely related to the purchasing solution is the assumption that bigger is always better. Sometimes when I am at a conference or an event where there are many pastors, we talk about our churches. When I tell people how many attend our church, the majority of them say, "Hang in there. It gets better." Few if any ask for context or where the church has been or what it has done or anything else. There seems to be an unspoken number below which a church is not successful. This notion is evident in where people attend, where ministers choose to serve, and how members and clergy alike perceive church leaders.

Learning in the Wilderness
Many of us are already deep into the wilderness of loss—the loss of members, cultural clout, and connection to the world around us. We have to learn as we go, something hard to do. There are no clear paths to follow in the wilderness. There are many strange noises, multiple ways forward, and myriad concerns in our minds. This wilderness is an inhospitable place that does not feel like home. Still, the wilderness is where we are and where we need to relearn the world around us. This journey will take us through places that we may perceive as hostile, but it will also likely lead to a world where the definition of growth itself is radically changed.

We often think of the wilderness as a place of trials, as with the ancient Israelites, or a place of desolation, such as when Jesus was tempted. However, Scripture offers another perspective about the wilderness. For example, the Gospel of Luke says of John the Baptist, "The child grew and became strong in spirit, and he was in the wilderness until the day he appeared publicly to Israel" (Luke 1:80, NRSV). Later accounts testify to what John became (cf. Luke 1:66): one who "appeared in the wilderness of Judea," preaching repentance that led to confession of sins, and above all proclaiming the coming of the Messiah (Matthew 3:1-12; Luke 3:1-20; John 1:19-28). For John the Baptist, the wilderness was a place of preparation that led to effective ministry.

In a similar way, time in the wilderness prepared Jesus for his ministry. The Gospels recount his forty days of fasting and temptation (Matthew 4:1-11; Luke 4:1-13). At the end of this time, "suddenly angels came and waited on him" (Matthew 4:11, NRSV). Luke's account adds, "Then Jesus, filled with the power of the Spirit, returned to Galilee, and a report about him spread through all the surrounding country. He began to teach in their synagogues and was praised by everyone" (Luke 4:14-15, NRSV).

This perspective suggests that the wilderness in which we find ourselves may be a place of learning and preparation for us instead of a barren land where we might die. If we are willing to examine ourselves with honesty and seek what God wants us to do, we may find that our churches again can provide effective ministry.

Asking the following questions may be a good beginning.

- Why do we need to go on this journey?
- Is our desire for moving now born out of our wish to preserve a place that we love?
- Have we looked at ourselves deeply enough?
- Do we have the energy for the journey? What resources do we have?
- Where should we go?

After answering questions like these that apply to our contexts, we then can explore our challenges from a deeper and broader perspective. When we know more about where we have been and where we are now, we may be able to see some of the reasons that have contributed to our arrival in this wilderness. Being more aware of where we are is a wonderful way to begin our process of response to the call in Matthew 28.

CHAPTER 3

Responding to Change

> All spoke well of him and were amazed at the gra-
> cious words that came from his mouth. They said, "Is
> not this Joseph's son?" (Luke 4:22, NRSV)

In Luke 4:14-30 the unknown world has come home to those listening to Jesus. The day started like any other as the people of
Nazareth prepared and went to synagogue. Once there, as far as
we can tell from the text, they found familiar faces—neighbors and
friends. Then suddenly someone they knew got up and began
speaking as though he had a right to hold the sacred Scriptures and
expound upon them. This young man wasn't the son of a rabbi.
He was the son of Joseph—yes, the carpenter! How dare he
assume he could do that? Quickly, all those in the synagogue found
themselves disoriented and far from home. Pause for a moment
and try to imagine the facial expression and inflection with which
people said, "Isn't this Joseph's son?"

The unknown had invaded their synagogue, and their first reaction was to grasp at something, anything, familiar to make sense of
what was happening. They realized that they knew the young man.
They knew his family and how the household earned a living. They
probably knew much more about Jesus and his family than his
father's name and family's trade. They had seen Jesus play with
their sons, or perhaps they had even been among those childhood
playmates. Yet, in this instance, all they knew about him could not
help them make sense of what was happening. At that moment all

their knowledge about Jesus only made things more complicated. In their highly structured society, they knew who he was and what he was supposed to do. Yet, he was not following any of the rules. They did not know how to react.

How many of us as leaders or as members of a congregation have found ourselves asking, "Isn't this Joseph's son?" when we encounter something that diverges from what our experience tells us it should be? Our response to encountering the unknown in the familiar tends to be knee-jerk and emotionally charged.

In chapter 2 of this book, we read about a man who had gone on a mission trip to help the members of a church build their sanctuary. However, when the materials arrived, they were cut according to the metric system. The unexpected change affected the man deeply enough to frustrate him, and the emotional reaction of a frustrated person is to make a value judgment: "The materials are in the *wrong* sizes." As we prepare for this journey, we must account for the fact that we all will be trying to make sense of the new through the lenses of our past.

Dilemmas for Leaders and Churches

Helping a congregation journey to a multicultural world is a tall order. A leader will need to guide a local church through a long journey that will take people far from where many of them are while never leaving home. For many congregations this journey is further than they have ever before ventured. At first the new emotional space may look like a wilderness filled with imagined and real dangers. Those real and imagined dangers affect all who travel there for the first time, in real physical and emotional ways. To complicate matters further, often the move is born out of necessity, as a matter of survival, so the inevitable stress is felt more deeply. In short, a leader charged with guiding a faith community into a multicultural world faces dilemmas that tend to be difficult to grasp and often offer no clear path through.

At the root of these difficulties is the fact that often the leader is in effect a guide into a world that she does not know either. Or, if the leader knows the new world well, then it is likely that she cannot see this place in the same way as do those she is guiding. In other words, the leader asks a congregation to go into an unknown wilderness while she is either as lost as they or is so far ahead that it becomes difficult to see the group's difficulties.

What is a leader to do? Should she offer certainties every chance she gets? Should she do her best to portray calm certainty about where the community is and where they are going? Can she show her uncertainty and still be an effective leader? Will the people still follow if they know the leader also is worried, uncertain, scared, and even lost at times? A shift so monumental can leave a leader confused and frustrated, and perhaps even suck all the hope out of her sails. All of this leads us to one of our central dilemmas: Can we risk much for the sake of a future that is yet unseen and thus unknowable? Or, should we go with what we know but with more energy and pray that God will see us through?

Walking in the deep jungle as a novice is a scary and frustrating experience. The jungle is so dense that one can barely see a few dozen yards ahead at best, and what is seen is just more of the same. For long stretches of time, then, all one has is either trust in the guide or whatever equipment the leader has (GPS, map, compass, etc.). In those journeys one often hears questions such as "How much longer?" "Which way do we go?" "When is sundown?"

An experienced guide will have answers for all those questions. "It will be a couple more hours until we rest." "We're headed south, toward that hill you see over there." "Don't worry, we'll be at camp with plenty of time to get settled before sundown." Those answers matter because they are reassuring, but they are also nothing without trust in the one who is saying them. Unlike an experienced guide, many of us in leadership will be asked those questions while we are in our first journey and still unsure ourselves of most of the answers.

A clarifying and sobering fact is that it is difficult to navigate in the unknown even when we have prepared to encounter it. If we have been thrown into the unknown unexpectedly, we may find ourselves on the verge of throwing Jesus off a cliff, just as the people from his hometown were prepared to do (Luke 4:29)!

At the root of our leadership dilemma is that the concept of an unknown place is difficult to explain in our current world. Few of us ever find ourselves in unknown places. If, for some reason, we are in an unfamiliar location, we carry with us tools that can help us dispel a good deal of the uncertainty and anxiety that come from not knowing. The smartphones that most of us carry can tell us where we are and how to get to where we are going. If we are hungry or need gas, we can run a simple search and be given dozens of options. Many phones can even translate foreign languages for us. So, most of our "Isn't this Joseph's son?" moments happen between us and our phones or computers, which leave us with an unrealistic perception of the unknown.

It may be tempting to praise the go-getter aspect of thinking that we on our own can access and absorb knowledge proficiently enough to use it appropriately. But in reality what many people end up with is an inflated sense of self, born out of a false certainty about their own capacity to navigate the unknown.

As that new reality of the unknown begins to sink in, we may be tempted to transfer into the emotional realm the false sense of security that our access to information gives us. We may even be tempted to extend our false sense of knowing into our problem-solving strategies when dealing with church and people. It seems that we have come to believe ourselves to be only a quick Google search away from knowledge and answers to most if not all questions.

There is access to so much information that leaders find themselves in charge of groups of people who think of themselves as competent at nearly anything or, worse, as experts in something that they have spent several hours looking up. We are faced with the difficult dilemma of having to convey the true, unsettling meaning of the unknown to people who are not even aware that they do not know. We have to find ways to explain how difficult change will be in the midst of unrealistic expectations of the self and those in charge. It is not an exaggeration to say that many leaders now face churches, groups, or organizations with people who expect nearly immediate and accurate information as well as equally fast and correct choice-making. How is a leader to guide a group that is overly confident in its ability to handle the unknown into what certainly is *terra incognita* in the sense of ancient cartography? (Go ahead. I'll be here waiting while you Google that.)

What follows are suggestions, examples, and directions for following God's calling as you embark on a journey into the unknown. Let us begin with some traveling guides for your journey.

Hope in a New Perspective

A first step in wrestling with this dilemma is to acknowledge that we probably have to go back further than expected in preparing ourselves and our people for change. In many ways we have to convince them that we are going into the unknown and that there is nothing we can do to get to know the place emotionally before going there. You see, many of us grow to assume that because we can physically navigate our world by using the myriad tools available, we can also use the same tools to navigate emotionally through an unknown world. However, the tools that help us get places physically are inadequate to help us through the emotional journey. So, our struggle as leaders in the beginning is not necessarily to define the meaning of multiculturalism and Christian diversity, as many in the congregation have probably read many things on it and have their own ideas. Rather, we need to prepare ourselves and our people by developing and creating tools that can help sustain us emotionally in the unknown world. To that end, we have to find ways to see our worlds from a different perspective in order to begin discovering what our own perspective is as we move toward a new place.

One day a father was at home with his five-year-old son. Dad was doing some work in the study next to the living room. This was during December, so dad was keeping his ears open even more than usual; the Christmas tree was already up, and there were gifts under it. Dad realized quickly that the living room had become quiet. Just as he was about to get up and see what was going on, he saw his son walk toward his bedroom. Curiosity awoken, dad turned his chair toward the hallway as he waited to see what would happen next.

Less than a minute later, he saw his son walk back toward the living room with purpose. Nearly immediately there was another trip. By now, dad's curiosity had been piqued. There were four such trips in the course of ten minutes. Then, all was quiet again. Dad couldn't wait any longer, so he got up and walked to the living room. He half expected to catch his son trying to sneak a peak at the gifts. Instead, what he saw in the living room upset him almost as much as it surprised him. He looked at the gifts, and they were all seemingly intact. With relief he looked up, and that's when he saw what his son had done to the tree.

The first thing he noticed was a rubber band on one of the branches. To the left of it was a crumpled-up piece of paper that looked like it had been rescued from the garbage. Things got worse as his gaze moved around a Christmas tree that now was full of garbage about as high as a five-year-old could reach. At this point, Dad was so angry that he needed someone to yell at, so he looked down to the left for his son. What he saw surprised him. His son did not look guilty as he usually did when he knew he was in trouble. Instead, his son was looking back at him with pride and a broad smile that melted dad's heart.

It wasn't long before anger returned to dad, and he said sternly, "Why have you done this to the tree?" He could tell by his son's surprised expression that he was missing something about what was happening. So, against every instinct to yell, he knelt down and asked as calmly as he could, "Why did you put these things on the tree?" His son replied, "Well, you told me that Christmas trees are put up to remind us of God and our family's love for us. Then, when we were adding things to it, you told me how all the things we put up were special reminders for us from family." By now, dad's anger was dissipating.

His son continued, "So, I was playing and looked at the tree and saw that I didn't give anything for it. So I went to my room for my special things." Dad said, "Special things?" The son, pointing at the crumpled paper, replied, "Yes, this is a picture of all of us I drew." (The paper was crumpled because the boy had been trying to carry too many things at the same time.) Pointing at something else, he said, "This is the wrapper of my favorite candy ever!"

For the next ten minutes dad heard an explanation from his son for every piece of garbage now on the tree. All of those things stayed on the tree for the Christmas season, and dad was ever ready and glad to explain, to anyone who asked, why these were the best Christmas tree decorations his family had ever had.

More often than we may be ready to accept, a change in perspective can and does change how we feel about something. In fact, frequently what needs to change is not the situation in which we find ourselves but the perspective that we have of it. A change of perspective for dad made what at first seemed like garbage into the greatest Christmas decorations ever. In a similar way, seeing diversity as proof of new life can become a powerful tool for our emotional journey. A change in perspective can be so powerful that it could bring as much comfort as suddenly recognizing a street when we're lost in an unknown place.

History and Tradition: Tools or Obstacles?

Many small congregations are in crisis because they have been unable to engage with the world as it has changed around them. In my younger years I worked as an exterminator during two summers. One client was a woman who had lived in the same apartment since the late 1940s. Her husband had passed away decades before I met her, and all her children had moved on to their own families in the suburbs. Yet, it seemed to me that this woman was unable to let go of that home, so she kept it as it was in the 1950s. To step into her house was to travel back in time. Everything was from that long-gone era—the stove, the icebox, the clock. If people from the 1950s had traveled to the future and landed in that apartment, they would have thought that their time machine was broken and had failed!

In a similar way, many of our local congregations refuse to let go of the good old days, so they remain in a sort of time capsule. They know how to function well in it; they know where everything is and how it works. This place is comfortable. It is home! These churches stay with the familiar while the world drifts even further away.

How a leader handles love for home as it is can influence greatly how the congregation decides to engage with the current world. But, the question still remains, how could a leader show people the good in a new world where, as far as the older members know, everything is worse than it was before? Is there a way to say that something is better without saying that what they know is bad? To push too hard could make the people feel that they are cheating on their past, especially since everything around them is being taken from them, and church is the one place where they can continue to be as they have been. Their church is the place they can continue to follow Christ in a faithful way that saw great success for the church while they were strong and active. Yet, not to push is a recipe for the closing of the church. A leader must deal with the dilemma of respecting and conserving what came before while working to transform the past and tradition into a tool to help the congregation take the risky leap forward into the unknown.

CHAPTER 4

Drawing Hope from
Our History

> For whatever was written in former days was written
> for our instruction, so that by steadfastness and by
> the encouragement of the scriptures we might have
> hope. (Romans 15:4, NRSV)

Before we dive into the hope and strength found in history, let us examine context briefly. In many congregations, history, success, and strength are closely related to similar physical aspects of the longest-term members. Currently, our oldest congregants tend to be a mix of the so-called Greatest Generation and Baby Boomers. Both groups saw great success during their adult lives. The Greatest Generation fought and won a world war overseas and worked hard back home to bring about success. The Baby Boomers were a physical growth from that success and the inheritors of great wealth.

Sadly, the decline in the North American church has, in many ways, coincided with these generations' decline in health and influence. It isn't too far-fetched to think that a good part of the refusal to change could be tied to who and how successful many of these people were when they were younger. They know that church works, and if only these new generations would work "as hard as we did," this thing can be turned around. So, consciously or unconsciously, they feel the load physically as well as psychologically.

If this context does not fit your particular situation, please spend some time working out your congregation's own context within a historical framework. All of us have a historical framework as individuals and as a faith community. Even recent church starts have to carry the weight of the history that its core group and new members bring with them. It is difficult to overestimate the importance of learning the contextual history of the church as part of the process that will lead to finding hope and strength in the past.

Proceeding from the framework above, we can now explore possible ways through which hope and strength are drawn from history.

History as Hope and Strength

Hope
Preparing to move to the unknown is a stressful process that can be greatly relieved by the hope that can come from the belief that good can and will come from the transition. In the story of Jesus' conversation with the rich young ruler (Matthew 19:16-22; Mark 10:17-22; Luke 18:18-23), a big part of the difficulty for this young man was that on first view, it looked like his move would have him be worse off than he was. He seems to have equated his wealth with his overall well-being—spiritually as well as economically. Removing the source of his well-being—his possessions—did not make sense to him. For this rich young man, there was no hope to be drawn from going without.

As the encounter with the rich young ruler illustrates, finding hope in the prospect of moving needs a transition into trusting that what is coming is good, and perhaps even better than where we are. The young man was unable to make that move because he trusted the law more than Jesus. We can use the rich young man as an example of what not to do. But by looking at the breadth of Scripture, we find examples of the hope found in difficult moves to the unknown. Moses' mother placed her child in a river with only hope about where he would drift (Exodus 2:1-10). Moses later was asked to return to the place where he was a fugitive to carry out an impossible task (Exodus 3:7-12). The child with a lunch and Andrew the apostle, who proposed the child's lunch as a solution to feeding the crowd (John 6:1-15), both moved to the unknown in hope.

In the early church, people turned to their leaders to resolve disputes and then acted on their advice (Acts 6:1-6), with the result that the "word of God continued to spread; the numbers of the disciples increased greatly in Jerusalem" (Acts 6:7, NRSV). As the gospel continued to spread (Acts 10), new questions arose from territory that was emotionally and (somewhat) geographically unfamiliar. Again, wise counsel guided believers (Acts 15). As Paul's epistles show, the questions continued to be raised, but the principles were in place and could be recalled for the believers' benefit.

Scripture reminds us that we can trust that God will deliver us because God has been delivering God's people for millennia. Of course, many times that deliverance comes in unexpected and uncomfortable ways. Let us explore some examples of how God's people have walked in trust with God. These examples can serve as steppingstones, principles that we can follow in this journey in the wilderness of the unknown.

A second source of hope from our past is that we have come this far as a church by learning from our mistakes and moving on from them. If life was nursed from the ashes of the worst war in history, we too can nurture our congregations back into life. The world is different now, but that mainly means that the set of difficulties that we face has changed. So, we need to spend time learning these new difficulties. When we learn what those difficulties are, we can set about creating responses that feed the intangible needs that are present throughout history.

Principles from Scripture

Good can come from a move to the unknown (Matthew 19:16-22; Mark 10:17-22; Luke 18:18-23). Walking can be made difficult simply by closing our eyes. If we cannot see ahead, our whole being worries and expects to hit something. Scripture is a reassuring, guiding voice to help us while we walk into the unknown.

Trust in God leads to extraordinary change (Exodus 2:1-10; 3:7-12). Trust is a powerful force that is fragile at the same time. It is easy to lose trust. But, by focusing on the fact that God is perfect, we can do the work to keep our trust alive even during the trials of the journey.

Hope helps us move toward the unknown (John 6:1-15). Hope is most needed when it seems most inappropriate. I wonder how each of us would have responded to Andrew when he showed up with one modest meal when the problem at hand was the feeding of thousands. He might not have known what was going to happen, but he hoped that Jesus would!

Believers turn to Spirit-led leaders and hear sound advice (Acts 6:1-6). Too often in times of crisis the loudest and most fear-filled voices are the ones heard. Scripture shows us time and time again how, if we wait to hear the Spirit, we will not be led astray.

People from different backgrounds hear the gospel and believe (Acts 10). God created diversity. We must follow God in our listening and learning, even if it comes from places we do not expect.

Leaders guided by God can give wise counsel that applies in new situations (Acts 15). Sometimes traditions are mere habits that we enforce for their own sake. Peter's words in Acts 15:7-11 came after much debate. It is important to listen and engage in order for us together to arrive at the heart of God's message for us here and now.

Theological Conclusion

Scripture reminds us that we can trust God to deliver us because God has been delivering God's people for millennia.

Everyone needs to feel welcomed, loved, encouraged, and supported. We all need to belong. However, events such as a night of square dancing at the church probably is not as effective a vehicle to convey these essentials now as it was before. But we know that the purpose for a square dance was precisely to share the intangibles discussed in the previous sentences. Changing the vehicle that carries this purpose does not mean that we have to change at the core. Where have we learned these principles from? We have come to know these essential needs through experience and help from our elders. Because our older congregants know about learning from those who have come before them, it becomes easier to show them that we now need them, as they are the elders from whom we can learn the essentials of life and church. We, as a congregation, have come far indeed by being willing and ready to learn.

Therefore, as we gather our own history, we can more clearly see that we can adjust to change. Any church that has existed for any significant amount of time has lived through having to make changes in order to adjust to different circumstances. In this sense, then, our history can be a source of hope when we look at instances during which we have successfully adjusted to changes. Looking at our history should also demonstrate to us that difficulty is an ever-present companion to change. So, this new change that includes a move to the unknown is more of the same but with a different set of difficulties.

In one congregation that I served, an elder congregant was not a fan of the changes being made. After chatting, we discussed specific instances of past change that he remembers pushing for at that church. After thinking for a while, he told me that when he was in youth group, they were tired of the old hymns and wanted to add some more contemporary music. They found a hymnal that had some newer songs but still had many of the great old hymns. He was part of the representative youth who dressed up, cut and combed their hair, and went to the deacons' meeting. Before they had even pleaded their case, the chair of the board told them that grownups know best and to leave church business to those responsible for caring for their spiritual well-being. This gentleman was left with a mixture of feelings that have affected his view of change in church all his life. Perhaps grownups were more qualified when it came to changes in church because it is related to spiritual matters and that needs maturity. Now that he is a grownup, shouldn't the younger people listen? He had to.

This man did not change his mind about the current changes there and then. But being reminded of a time when he was pushing for change helped him get started on his own journey into the unknown. He did not come to love the changes, but he found that he had less and less energy to spend in opposing the change. That energy then was put to use in other aspects of church life.

Another part of finding hope in the past is recognizing that history does happen in cycles. As Mark Twain is reputed to have said, "History doesn't repeat itself, but it does rhyme." When I was in high school, one of my good friends was part of the yearbook committee. One day I asked him how they had decided on the "new and cool" design of the yearbook. He said, "We looked at yearbooks from the 1950s and 1960s and took little parts from many of them. Then we made them cooler."

Each new generation thinks of itself as more trailblazing than the previous one, and each decade has its own descriptor for that quality, whatever makes it more "ripping" (1910s), "solid" (1930s), "groovy" (1960s), "cool" (1980s), or "phat" (1990s). Likewise, as it ages, each generation grows in contempt for and anxiety about the new ones. However, the knowledge that the old can become the new with a few adjustments can become a powerful source of hope. History does not repeat itself, but it certainly rhymes.

Strength

One of the most mismanaged resources of a local church is its history. I have often heard of "tradition" (which is frequently used as a synonym for "history") as being one of change's greatest enemies. Many leaders prejudge tradition and the history of a place as a negative force or dead weight that must be avoided until one is strong enough to fight it into extinction. In fact, I have found that tradition is one of the most common obstacles named by leaders endeavoring to lead an organization toward change.

However, as leaders, we cannot avoid contending with history and tradition. A very important part of life in community is the gathered knowledge, experiences, prejudices, difficulties, good memories, and many more "things" that we place under the umbrella of tradition or history. These factors are too important to ignore or discard. This collection is a powerful force actively affecting the community, and the effects of this action are felt all over said community.

So, what can a leader do when facing such an amassing of power that is ever ready to react and capable of winning most of the time?

The first step is what I have discussed: to acknowledge that there is power in tradition and history. It cannot be avoided, and fighting it is often a fool's errand. Those of us sold on bringing about change can easily be prejudiced against tradition to such extent that we become what we are fighting. For example, there is the notion that everything about new, young churches must not look like a traditional church. The front of "modern" sanctuaries looks less like a traditional church chancel and more like a secular concert stage, with its dedicated band space, theatrical lighting, and hi-tech audio-visual setup. This new standard is so popular that "churchy-looking" sanctuaries are disdained as old-fashioned and wrong. The past is seen in such a bad light that we think that a full split with it is what change means. We begin to see no good side to living within the history of a place and carrying the tradition with us into the new world to which we are traveling. Worse, because we see it as something that has contributed to the crisis that we are living, many of us, in self-deception, attack it. We are certain that we must prevail before change begins. The result often is pain that does much damage. Be prepared to acknowledge the power of history and tradition for the sake of your leaders as well as the congregation.

Once we have identified the power of history, the next step is to get to know it. In order to engage with this part of the journey of discovery, the leaders need to do a cleansing self-check. Remember: history and tradition are our antagonist, the nemesis in our story, and we may be surprised by how much we cannot see because of our prejudices and pride. Take an inventory of where you feel the power of tradition and history resides in the system. Then check your perceptions against the lived reality of the place. How close are you to the lived reality and relationship of the church with its past? Knowing well where power is wielded will be helpful as you encourage all to move forward in the journey.

Then, take a step back and observe how the system has responded to change. Visit with those who have lived through a long period of that history. What is salient? Which events affected the congregation most? Whom do they hold responsible for these changes? Why are things done the way they are? Who initiated those traditions? Take it all in, create a record of all these details, become a student of the past to deepen your knowledge of the place and the events that gave birth to the traditions held so dearly by those who are still around. All of that learning is important in order to lead this group into the difficult journey toward faith-based multiculturalism. We need to learn our community's past as deeply as possible. The life that has been lived holds a special and powerful place in the psyche of the group; it cannot be ignored and certainly not antagonized as irrelevant or no longer useful.

The more steeped you become in the history and tradition of the church, the better you will see the power that resides there. That power, when wielded in a healthy way, can be the force that propels the church toward the new land of Christian diversity. However, too often this power is either wasted or mismanaged. We tend to use the methods that were effective before when what we need to use is the journey that led to those methods being such creative and effective responses in their time.

It is a common misconception that churches always close because of a lack of resources. In fact, most local churches have closed after a considerable expenditure of plentiful but mismanaged energy and resources.

Perhaps now would be a good time to see how resources have been used (and misused) in your particular context. Think of the strategies, programs, and all attempts that were made by the congregation that you are leading. What was the process that led your group to that particular attempt at reaching out to new life? Which were the fears and worries that affected how that initiative was carried out? What was the long-term plan for each particular program? Were the discussions during planning focused on how much this initiative could yield as far as new people or funds or on how well it responded to the learned needs in the neighborhood? How did the group go about seeking to discern the leading of the Spirit?

I am aware that words such as "mismanage," "misuse," and "waste" sound harsh, particularly in a place like a church under stress. Therefore, the leader would do well to use such terms judiciously in public. However, self-examination requires us to have as candid a look inward as possible. Preparing for the journey to come needs honesty and clarity in discussing our good attributes as well as our failures.

We should also remember that mismanagement and waste are not always done intentionally or out of neglect or incompetence. All of us waste resources constantly. All too often I have turned on the hot water in the shower and let it run for several minutes before I realized it. Of course, when it comes to church life, many of us have a difficult time exploring failures or mistakes. Yet, in spite of our best wishes, most of the energy wasted in a church environment is squandered with the best of intentions. Many congregations do indeed bend over backwards for the sake of their church and those outside with no visible results.

Part of this discussion regarding history has to include a frank review of what waste consists of and the extent to which we have mismanaged resources. This will be a painful discussion that could lend itself to airing grudges. There are resources to deal with difficult issues in a church environment (the list at the end of this chapter includes some examples). However, it will be difficult to move forward without a clear and deliberate discussion on how we have been using our resources up to this point.

An example is that of a church on its way to death. Its attendance had dwindled to about twenty people from a peak of one thousand on Sunday mornings. After discussion, someone brought up the fact that there were many children in the church's neighborhood, so the church decided to start a game night on Saturday evenings. The event was announced around the neighborhood and for several weeks through the church's usual channels as well. The first game night finally arrived, and there were fifteen people in attendance.

What follows are some of the comments from the leaders as they gathered to assess the event. These comments are clearly an exploration of the many ways in which the leaders thought that the event failed. Now, objectivity can be a moving target, but let's consider the comments.

"All of the people there were from the church." This idea had touched on something special for those attending the church. The church had just fed its congregation.

"I don't understand why we had only fifteen people there." The church's attendance was about twenty people on Sunday morning, so three-quarters of the church's Sunday morning attendees were there on a Saturday night. Almost the entire church showed up!

"There wasn't much interaction between the generations." The first event was already intergenerational and thus multicultural! (Even within ethnic groups, you often find different cultures across generations where first-generation folks may speak a different language and preserve traditions and values from the country of origin.) What a great beginning on the journey toward cultivating Christian diversity!

"Only half the people there were young." So, nearly half of those attending the church event were young people? Please tell me what you did! I would love that percentage of youth at our events. All of these good things happened even though it was the first time the event was held. Yet, the Saturday night game nights were canceled and chalked up as yet another failure.

This example illustrates how easy it is to waste resources when we are blinded by urgency or unrealistic expectations. The church was on to something, yet the program was canceled because it did not meet the specific hopes that the church had for it on the first night. The perception of limited resources led this church to end something too soon. Who knows what would have happened if the game nights had continued? They had stumbled upon a great opportunity that only needed a little more time to show its worth. Plus, the church had plenty of resources to give that ministry the time it needed. There was buy-in from the congregation; nearly all of them attended the first event. Yet, because the history of the church had seen eight hundred children enrolled in Sunday school, fifty men at men's group, and countless other large groups, fifteen people seemed like a failure in comparison. Their anxiety from living in crisis probably moved them to kill new life that had been well planted.

So, a rich history is a double-edged sword. It can be a source of steady hope, or it can become a weight that drags behind, especially when things get difficult. Many leaders, perhaps sensing the difficulty, sidestep this powerful force as much as they can. There is another option: a clean break with the past. Scrapping the past works only if the plan is to start from scratch. But if that is the plan, then one must expect that the current church will die.

To harness the strength and presence of the history of a place is an essential task for leaders who are journeying through the wilderness and toward diversity in community. It is the task of the leader to discern how this power is best wielded. As I noted earlier, in many instances the lack of resources is more a perception than the reality of the situation. The task, then, is to help those we are leading to walk the long and arduous path toward rechanneling their strengths. Doing so will help bring renewed life within the new context of diversity.

Lastly, I have found that the level of difficulty in the journey is directly related to the amount of experience the person has. The more experienced the persons, the more difficult it will be for them to undertake the journey that will lead to new or different ways of using their resources. It would be wonderful if your context were the direct opposite of mine. However, if that were the case, I dare say that you would not be reading these words.

As we near the end of this chapter I hope you find that there is much cause for joy as we find ourselves discussing how best to harness already existing resources rather than where to find help with limited means. If it is harnessed in a helpful way, the power that comes from history and corporate memory can become the strength needed to help the group make it through the difficult journey and through the early days in an unfamiliar multicultural world.

Resources for Reconciliation and Transformation

Beazley, Hamilton. *Reclaiming the Great Commission: A Practical Model for Transforming Denominations and Congregations.* San Francisco: Jossey-Bass, 2000.

DeYoung, Curtiss Paul. *Coming Together in the Twenty-First Century: The Bible's Message in an Age of Diversity*. Valley Forge, PA: Judson Press, 2009.

———. *Reconciliation: Our Greatest Challenge—Our Only Hope*. Valley Forge, PA: Judson Press, 1997.

Friend, Howard E., Jr. *Recovering the Sacred Center: Church Renewal from the Inside Out*. Valley Forge, PA: Judson Press, 1998.

Laubach, David C. *12 Steps to Congregational Transformation: A Practical Guide for Leaders*. Valley Forge, PA: Judson Press, 2006.

Ott, E. Stanley. *Twelve Dynamic Shifts for Transforming Your Church*. Grand Rapids: Eerdmans, 2002.

CHAPTER 5

Discerning a True Sense of Belonging

> Sell all that you own and distribute the money to the poor, and you will have treasure in heaven; then come, follow me. (Luke 18:22, NRSV)

Who we are is at least partially dependent on who we are not. Admittedly, most of us do not think of ourselves in terms of who we are not. However, our brain helps us understand the world around us in part by identifying how we differ from others. It is important to note that it takes time and experiences with others to develop a clearer sense of those differences. Therefore, who we are, our sense of identity, is substantially rooted in the accumulation of what we have lived.

Who we are owes much to a collected, messy, rich combination of memories, assumptions, prejudices, opinions, and much more. Most people rarely think about what makes us who we are, and much less do we parcel our sense of identity into smaller components so we may understand it better. Because many people have not given much thought about their identity, we need to guide those we are leading toward a deeper understanding of their identity by a roundabout way. We will begin by exploring our personal sense of belonging by exploring how we perceive ourselves to be is influenced by our relationship to those around us. The meaning of belonging serves as an entryway to broadening our understanding of our identity. Asking our congregation to think about where they belong can be a fruitful first step in preparing for our journey toward Christian diversity.

A Sense of Self

In the encounter recorded in Luke 18:18-25, we are introduced to a young man of wealth and position who seems to know very well who he is and what he needs to do to be a follower of Christ. This knowledge brings this young man a sense of clarity and confidence. His response to Jesus indicates that he feels that he has already done what needs to be done for the journey to come. The young man is emboldened and probably even eager to get started. He is different from the disciples by virtue of the fact that he chooses to approach Jesus. (Conversely, the Gospels record that nearly all of the disciples chosen by Jesus were approached by him.) Then, when Jesus gives him a requirement, he seems to be neither hesitant nor intimidated. To Jesus' statement about following the commandments the young man replies, "I have kept all these since my youth" (Luke 18:21, NRSV).

When I read this story, I can almost see the young man walking tall toward Jesus. He is ready to ask his question so that he will receive public confirmation of what he already knows to be the truth. And Jesus' response was exactly what the young man was ready to answer: "I have kept all these [commands] since my youth." Then Jesus says, "There is still one thing lacking" (Luke 18:22, NRSV).

I can almost again see the young man's face—he is ready for the next challenge. Yet, by the end of Jesus' comment on what he is lacking, he has been deflated. "Sell all that you own and distribute the money to the poor, and you will have treasure in heaven; then come, follow me"—this is too far for this young man to go. Rather than seek to learn to change, he retreats. He knows where he belongs and what is required of him in order to move on to the next step in discipleship. However, his certainty about his identity is so well established and solid that when Jesus deviates from the plan, he cannot follow the change. The young man has come to know his "faith" so well that he has no room for following.

We don't know from this passage the precise reason why the young man was unable to follow Jesus. Was it a purely selfish decision to turn away? Or did he have family members or servants for whom he was responsible? It is clear that Jesus' request for him to leave behind what he loved was unexpected.

Like the young man in Luke, there are wonderful churches that have done their best to follow God since their beginning. In this spirit, congregations call out to Jesus that they are ready to follow, for they are secure in the knowledge of their previous faithful hard work. Like the rich young ruler, however, when these churches hear Jesus say, "There is still one thing lacking," they find themselves unable to continue to follow Jesus.

I interviewed a pastor whose church found itself unable to follow when Jesus changed the plan. When the pastor first came to the church in 2005, as part of his orientation, the building committee members told him that the church doors were locked five minutes after worship started on Sunday mornings. When he asked them why, the chair of the committee replied, "There are all kinds of people in this neighborhood now. In 1999 Clara had her purse stolen from the room closest to one door." The man said this with obvious seriousness and concern. As with the young man, the faith this church had was more focused on their current efforts and what they had done in the past than on following Jesus' leading. This particular congregation could have chosen to learn how to follow in a new way. Instead, like the young man who encountered Jesus and chose to retreat, the church knew its "faith" (its own local and insular version of Christian belief and practice) so well that it was unable to follow.

Why is it that our faith often gets in the way of following? This challenge may be that because our faith is so close to our heart our sense of self invades our faith thoroughly, to the point that faith and self become one. Therefore, there are times when our eager readiness to follow Jesus comes to a sudden stop because we may feel that we are asked to not be ourselves anymore. We have come to know our faith so well that Jesus should listen. It seems to me that the routinely neglected connection between our sense of identity and our faith has much to do with this difficulty. When the self and faith are undistinguishable, it can become difficult to follow because it means risking who we are.

A Sense of Belonging

We don't know what the young ruler who encountered Jesus did with the rest of his life. But we do know what many congregations have done when they have found themselves unable to follow. When our identity is at risk, most of us respond by closing in and guarding whatever we feel is threatened by the change. Our churches become rigid shelters for the good old days rather than living organisms for exploring new days. Our doors are locked for much longer than they are open in order to prevent the unknown, unfamiliar (and therefore "bad") element from walking in. Our worship styles often shelter us from the uncertain newness of the world—even the innovations of the church 2.0. The ministries that we carry out or attempt to start are those that worked well during the good old days. So, we go on with these ministries in constant confusion as to why people don't come. To top it all off, we signal to people who do not yet belong that they are not part of us by how they are treated when they do visit.

I recently went to a funeral at a church in my neighborhood. I was looking forward to the passing of the peace so I could meet people. There were six older women in the pew in front of me. I always enjoy talking with grandmotherly types, so I felt that I was in the perfect spot. However, when the time came for passing the peace, each of them in turn looked back at me. When they realized that they did not recognize me, each of them gave me a tiny smile and went on greeting one another. I had invaded their shelter; in me they saw an uninvited stranger who probably had come in right off the street. My presence in their church on that special funeral day was more a reason to worry than to rejoice. A shelter can be a refuge that protects or a place of escape that excludes.

It is only natural to seek refuge when we feel threatened, whether the threat is real or imagined. As far as a refuge goes, few places feel as safe and comfortable as a home where we belong.

The world around us has changed so much that many of us would live in despair if it weren't for church shelters where we can belong. This human need for belonging is the reason for clubs, teams, lodges, nationalism, racism, gangs, and just about any other group. The reason is not difficult to discern: belonging gives us a sense of grounding, protection, and comfort. When we know we belong and have that belonging affirmed by those around us, then we feel a foundation under our feet. Belonging also provides us with parameters and a world from which we can discern the broader universe around us. In many ways this sense of being helps us learn who we are and who we are not.

Who Am I?

God created us all as equal (Acts 17:24-27) while at the same time unique and distinct unto our individual selves (Psalm 139:13-16). However, as unique as we ourselves may feel, we all have an intrinsic need to connect with others in deeper senses than casual encounters. Such need drives us to seek out commonality with those around us, and the desire for intimacy may be what drives us toward creating distinctions between groups. In his poem "We and

They," Rudyard Kipling wrote, "All nice people, like Us, are We, and everyone else is They." We all want to be where we belong.

A journey into a diverse and multicultural world could seem to challenge or risk diluting our *us*-ness, that sense of belonging that underpins so much of our world. In order to prepare for such a radical journey, it behooves a leader and the congregation to explore how the individual and community live out their us-ness.

Now is a good time to explore some of our own sense of belonging as individuals, so here is an exercise. Take a pen and paper (or another device for recording information) and compose a few words or sentences about where you feel you belong. It would be good to think of it in a socio-ethnic sense. Perhaps the following questions can help you guide this process.

■ Where do you feel you belong socially? (I have left this question intentionally broad to help you explore more freely.)

■ How did you arrive at the decision regarding where you belong?

■ To what extent was your family a strong source of information for your decision? What about your last name?

■ How would you define your ethnicity?

■ How much did the color of your skin influence your definition of your ethnicity? What about your cultural preferences?

■ How foundational was the influence of the place where you were born?

A note of caution: resist the temptation to provide Sunday school answers, answers such as "We all belong to the human race," "There is only one race," "We are all equal children of God," "I am a good Christian," "I don't see color or race." Let's remember that if Sunday school answers were entirely true as the source of our sense of belonging in our world, then there would be no need for books like this one.

Pay attention to issues such as family belonging, ethnicity, place of origin, place of birth (if different from origin), and any others along that line. It would be great if you could go deeper than these examples, such as asking how it is that you define your own ethnicity. What about yourself tells you that you belong in your racial or ethnic group? Explore the assumptions that you may be making about these questions. For example, people of German origin in Argentina may look like a typical German American yet have little in common with any American beyond skin color and name.

When you are satisfied with the thoroughness of your response, leave it aside for a good while. When you return to what you wrote, that is the time to explore your answers and ask "Why?" of each of them. The intent of this process is to help you explore why you feel you belong. There is no need for judgment during this part of the process, as the aim is to discover where you are, not where you should be.

In the end, you have arrived at a definition of belonging. We humans have an inherent need to know we belong. This belonging needs to be deeper than what our job, place, residence, or passport can provide. We all need to have identifiable markers that help us define the borders of the place we belong. It follows, then, that in order to have borders, there must be places beyond them. So, who we are is deeply related to how differentiated we are from others.

There is nothing wrong with acknowledging differences and how they affect us. A definition of where we belong based in part on exclusion is not in itself wrong. What we do with our sense of belonging when encountering the other is where we broaden our sense of identity. The broadening of our identity is never easy and is often painful. To open up our sense of identity in this way should not be done lightly or alone. We have noted the importance of trusting God through this journey, and moments like this one are precisely where that trust can sustain us as we move to the other side.

Home Is Where I Belong

Belonging is a deep, implicit sense of being a part of something in a way that is attached to the core of our being. Belonging is an essential part of our sense of well-being. Conversely, we also tend to see what belongs to us as defining characteristics of our identity and well-being. The young rich man (Matthew 19:16-22; Mark 10:17-22; Luke 18:18-23) was asked to give up what made up a large part of who he thought himself to be, not only in terms of donating his finances and property but also in terms leaving his family and friends—his home. The unsettling aspect of giving up his sense of belonging, along with his particular view on faith, kept him from following Jesus.

The exterior expression of many components of belonging (property, possessions, people), then, can be described as home. Through the following four concepts we can give a broad definition of home:

> a place I know
> where I am known
> where I know others
> where I know the language and traditions

A place I know. A calming effect happens when we are in a place we know well. It is comforting to be in a familiar place where we do not need directions to navigate the neighborhood or help in finding what we need in the kitchen. Home is good, and it is good to be home. Contrast that feeling of comfort, peace, and familiarity with how uncomfortable it can be to find yourself far from home. Think of the last time you traveled to a location you did not know. How did you feel driving, walking, or taking public transportation anywhere in that strange place? Even with turn-by-turn GPS navigation or directions from a resident, there is still a level of anxiety during those rare times we leave home. We are habitual beings who struggle with the new. If we become so comfortable at our home that we never venture out, it will make *a place I know* a home with no room for growth.

Where I am known. The beloved television sitcom *Cheers* was famous for its theme song, which described the comfort of a place where "everybody knows your name, and they're always glad you came." Many comforts come with being known. It feels great to walk into a place, be greeted by name, and see that others are clearly glad you are there. In such a place you find shared experiences, troubles, likes, and dislikes. People know you like family, and belonging there feels like home. Small churches offer that sense of family, of familiarity, of knowing you intimately. But, those congregations often also suffer anxiety about survival because of their smallness. So, when someone new comes, that person is welcomed in a way that says, "Welcome—do we have use for you!" The sense of gladness at being wanted is dissipated by the feeling of being wanted for what one brings, not who one is.

Where I know others. Conveniently, to be known can also mean to know. When we were in the process of adding a second bathroom at home, I needed to install the toilet. I had never installed one and did not feel comfortable doing it by myself. But I knew that my friend had just installed one at his home, so I called him to come over and help me. It is not rocket science to install a toilet, but that is beside the point. What was wonderful was knowing that someone I trusted was willing to walk with me through this new experience. In order to know people enough to trust them to guide or walk alongside us through the new, we need to have spent time with them in the old. In other words, it is always easier to ask for help when we know the people around us and are known by them.

Where I know the language and traditions. Two of the most difficult things about traveling are encountering different languages and traditions. "Language" does not refer only to speaking Spanish or French Creole or American Sign Language. Each place has its own linguistic distinctions, with variations of dialect or in specific vocabulary or jargon. But additionally, differences in language are related to shared experiences and contexts known only to "insiders," those for whom a place is home. For example, several years ago my brother called me and said, "My car broke down on 52nd and Broadway." I exclaimed, "What!?" His response was, "I know!" Now, you undoubtedly understood all of those words. You could even infer that there is something significant about that intersection. But whether it was good or bad, funny or dangerous, would depend on specific knowledge of that place—and possibly of my family! When you are home, shared language adds to a sense of belonging; but when you are away from home, differences in language can mean getting lost in translation.

Traditions are often activities that support the shared communal aspects of belonging. And where language encompasses both text and subtext, traditions are often unspoken altogether. For example, a Latino church in New Jersey is located in a changing neighborhood that is now a young, diverse professional community. In that congregation, everyone knows that every Communion Sunday there is dessert after church and that Señora Maria organizes it. This fellowship time is one of the most important community-building activities in that church. But nobody talks about it; it isn't in the bulletin, nor is it announced during worship. So, a visitor could visit for several months without knowing about it and thus would miss out on a great fellowship opportunity.

In this example, tradition is a wonderful thing that feeds community—literally and figuratively! Yet, the way it is handled by that community takes away from them rather than shows the world an example of the deep way they live out community. Language and tradition enhance the sense of belonging and facilitate the move of a place or building from just space to a place to call home. Knowing the local language and tradition goes a long way toward helping us feel at home.

Home as a Protective Shell

As wonderful as home is, we should do our best to remember that boundaries and borders are not ends unto themselves. There must be places and people beyond those borders with whom we can become *us*, but the way many of us frame our world based on race or citizenship creates a protective shell around us.

In some important ways this shell looks like many of our churches. The church has solid stone walls with only small entrances here and there. Beyond that entrance there is normally an entry room that is familiar and even personal to those who belong there. If your building is new, then its entry is likely an open foyer with colorful bulletin boards covered in event announcements and neatly labeled mail slots for "resident" staff. If your building is older, then the entry is a narthex, featuring stained glass given by someone's great-grandparents. This stained glass is directly above the podium donated by the men's Sunday school class of 1954 that holds the visitors' book.

Then yet another set of doors open into the sanctuary, which often is treated like the master bedroom of a home. It takes a deep level of familiarity with someone in order to feel comfortable in such a private place. Very few people can come into our bedrooms and sit on our bed to chat. And few guests feel comfortable while they are in our spiritual master bedroom, the sanctuary of our church. Those who eventually feel comfortable do so only after a long time and because of deep communal ties. Belonging does create a strong shell with an impressive set of protections.

These protections help us feel comfortable, safe, and warm. When we are faced with the other inside our shell, in a way that would make her or him more than just a visitor, it can feel like the warmth and protection that we have counted on while at home is being challenged. We all know that it is one thing to step out willingly, but it is completely different for that to be demanded of us. As a leader, then, one must be careful about how these protections are dealt with. Our shell can quickly go from being a refuge for those in need to a fortress protecting the ancient family who inherited it.

Because we have come to identify our sense of belonging with external factors, when we perceive a challenge to those traditions, institutions, and structures, we feel a need to preserve that identity more acutely. Opening up the places where we know we belong (and which we feel belong to us) can change things so much that we fear losing our place in the world that has been home.

Whether the danger of losing home is real or imagined matters little to someone who is experiencing the anxiety and worry of it. Sometimes opening up a place as intimate as our church can be difficult and worrisome because church is home in a profound way. To talk about opening up to a diverse and multicultural world is tantamount to allowing strangers to get comfortable in our master bedroom. We are reluctant to let the stranger "intrude" into one of the few places where we feel secure and protected.

When we encounter strangers in our home before we are ready to receive them, our response often comes from a sense of scarcity. Many of us react to new people as though home in the spiritual sense were as limited as home in the literal sense. Nobody would like a stranger to walk into the living room and say, "Hi. I live here now, so we need to make room." That would feel presumptuous at best and threatening and unsafe at worst.

Similarly, congregations begin to fear loss of our home, our safe place, our shelter, as soon as we perceive that *they* may be wanting to stay. So we are tempted to do something about it, and because we can no longer maintain homogeneity or enforce compliance with our status quo, we tend to sabotage the process of opening up our church home to others. Few places are as good at keeping people away as a church that is worried about losing its identity.

A while back, we at Calvary Baptist Church decided to make a leap of faith by moving our service from its sacred 10:45 a.m. time to 9:30 a.m. This meant that we could begin a new service for the new community around our walls as a sign of appreciation to them. Our choice came after noticing what happened when a church nearby started a Latino ministry by bringing others from the outside and *allowing* them to meet in the fellowship room in the afternoons. In no time there were two distinct groups, and the relationship was more of a landlord church to a tenant congregation than that of a church family.

In any case, we decided to start a new service with four people, one being the pastor and a second a volunteer church member. After months with only four to eight people in attendance, the service was finally growing. By the spring, after nearly a year of work, thirty people were regularly attending. As the summer approached, the church leaders met to decide what would happen in the summer months. Traditionally, the congregation had one service at 9:30 a.m. and no church school or other activities. So, the vote was to move again to one service at 9:30 a.m.

The attendees of the later service were informed that everyone was to worship together during the summer. However, no one mentioned that the combined service would not include an integration of worship styles. The church would worship in the tradition of the earlier service for the summer. By the end of July, very few people from the later service were showing up, and by the time the regular schedule resumed in September, none of those people were attending anymore. The church had to start again from the beginning. The later service eventually recovered, but none of the initial thirty people came back.

None of the leaders who voted to go to one service during the summer did it with the intention to end the later service. But it was growing fast in numbers and influence and beginning to take up more and more room at home. Perhaps unconsciously, we tried to teach them how to do church the "right" way by having them come to a "real" worship service, but instead we ended up losing them all. I think that this story illustrates how, more often than we would like, our local churches tend to be better at making choices that drive people away than at finding ways to broaden our sense of home.

What Do We Do?

By now in the book, as well as the church in general, we have lived with changes toward multiculturalism for a while, and one of the benefits of such change is that we now have some examples of how to approach change. For the rest of this chapter we will look at how megachurches seem to have dealt with the issue. We will then move to a broader and general look based on archetypes developed by the theologian Miroslav Volf.

In an extensive article in 2010, *Time* magazine reported on the multicultural nature of megachurches.[1] The article did its best to show how these churches were leading the way in racial reconciliation within the evangelical Christian world. Such an assertion is important, because faith communities continue to be some of the most segregated spaces in our country. However, I see a fundamental flaw in the article's assertion of multiculturalism as understood by its look at megachurches. At the core of my argument is a concept from anthropology known as Dunbar's Number. This concept states that a community of 150 members is the largest collection of people with whom any one individual can maintain meaningful relationships.

Another problem with mega-congregations being considered as an example of multicultural growth in church is clearly illustrated by Allan Aubrey Boesak and Curtiss Paul DeYoung in their book *Radical Reconciliation*: "Many multicultural and multiracial congregations are guided by a sensibility that reflects the white dominant culture of the United States."[2] In other words, in addition to large numbers of people making it easier for us to be at the same place while not relating to one another, we also fall into a new kind of homogeneity, assimilating anonymously into the majority culture.

Our sense of intimacy and belonging shifts as a greater number of people gather. Also, the focus of belonging shifts in a related way: the greater the number of people, the less we can see who is gathered with us and the more we focus on what we all gathered to see. The larger group dynamic is more likely to produce spectators than participants; it is more likely to invite reaction than engagement.

In terms of ethnic or cultural diversity, what happens at megachurches might be compared to a professional sports event. A sampling from most major sporting events would yield a fairly diverse group of people. However, it is unlikely that any person in attendance would know anyone seated even two rows away unless the individuals came together. Of course, everyone at the game or match is civil for the most part. All of them are present to cheer for their team; but when the event is over, people go their own separate ways. Similarly, in many of the megachurches, thousands are in the same place at the same time for the same purpose, but they may never know the name of a person seated three seats away.

So, multiculturalism on a mega scale does not challenge the protective shells of belonging our smaller communities create. In a large crowd we're not inviting the other into our bedroom; we're simply convening in the foyer or maybe the formal living room at the same time. In contrast, the smaller the number, the more difficult it is to live with diversity because the relative intimacy of proximity is perceived to challenge directly our sense of belonging. It forces questions about what it means to belong and the exclusivity that accompanies such sense of belonging. In other words, pushing for multiculturalism without a deep, comfortable sense of self can threaten the protective shell that belonging provides us.

Something has to be done as we engage the other in a deeper sense, because we all know that we live in a multicultural society. In his book *Exclusion and Embrace*, Miroslav Volf offers three general options that communities are often tempted to take in their pursuit of becoming a welcoming community:

Universalist option: We should control the unchecked proliferation of differences and support the spread of universal values. Places that follow this approach are ones where the focus is on our similarities at the expense of our diversity. The emphasis is on how we are all human who love, laugh, cry, and so on.

Communitarian option: We should celebrate communal distinctives and promote heterogeneity, placing ourselves on the side of the smaller armies of indigenous cultures. The places that follow this approach live in a constant struggle to highlight the differences between us all. In these places language is vigorously enforced to account for each distinct group. People wear their ethnic garb, and all sing in as many languages as possible.

Postmodern option: We should flee both universal values and particular identities and seek refuge from oppression in the radical autonomy of individuals. This type of congregation would do its best to eliminate any oppressive language from its speech and written materials so as to not undermine any individual sensitivity. These communities tend to remain in platitudes such as "love for all" and emphasize the importance of honoring all opinions at the expense of confronting the difficulties of depth in life together in the midst of differences.[3]

Each of these options has at least some appeal. There are churches that focus on what we have in common. The universalist option does seem appealing, especially because we all have a great deal of things in common. However, this view runs the risk of undermining the richness that can come from sharing in and benefiting from diversity and variety. Focusing on our differences alone, as the communitarian option shows, is also not enough. In this environment we run the risk of living as small, fragmented communities who share a space every once in a while. The postmodern option, in which everyone is a universe unto themselves that must be equally respected by all, can turn a church into a place where depth in community is forsaken under the shallow banner of respect for the other.

Life in Solidarity

In his book, Volf presents a fourth category: solidarity.[4] There is a word in Spanish, *acompañamiento*, that speaks to solidarity in the sense that Volf explores. *Acompañamiento* is not clicking "like" on a link or walking in a 5K fundraiser. Instead, solidarity (*acompañamiento*) is walking alongside someone else wherever that person may be. It means that one is exposed to the same things that the other person is experiencing, suffering as he or she suffers. When the great rabbi Abraham Joshua Heschel walked alongside Martin Luther King Jr. in protest, he said, "I felt my legs were praying." Heschel's legs were leading him toward being exposed to everything that King and the other protesters were suffering.

Solidarity expressed in this deeper sense does not eliminate the concerns that give rise to the three categories described by Volf. Instead, living in solidarity can move these concerns to a more appropriate place; they can be moderated by relationship. The deeper the relationship, the more room there is for living with differences as well as enjoying commonly shared aspects of life. Solidarity can place you fully on someone's side without having to become that person or forcing that person to become you.

A Baptist Filipino church in New Jersey welcomed a group of Hungarian Baptists who wanted a place to worship. Each community preferred to worship in its own language but chose to create spaces during the week where they could get to know each other.

There was nothing too involved about their communal times. They would share a meal or watch a soccer game together. There were no well-crafted programs or well-researched, culturally appropriate activities. These two groups simply spent time together.

Like many other churches, the Filipino church had a Wednesday prayer meeting. These meetings had been going on since before the Hungarians arrived. One day, as the prayer meeting was about to start, a group of the Hungarian church people showed up, saying that they were there for the prayer meeting. They hadn't called ahead to let the Filipino organizers set up or translate the prayer list. The Hungarian group assumed that because they were coming to the church, they were welcome at the prayer meeting. The Filipino members were suddenly asked to share their very intimate prayer time with the other without forewarning. Not only that, but the whole point of the prayer meeting was to learn about and pray for church members. So, the long-term members were going to have to pray in English, because that was the common language between the two groups.

This event would have been perhaps too tough to handle had they not already opened the space for deeper community by spending time together. It was those open times of fellowship that led the Hungarian group to feel welcomed and at home enough to just show up. Likewise, it was the open sharing that led the Filipino church members to welcome and include the other into yet another intimate space at home.

The church's leaders were instrumental in making the space necessary for that first prayer group to become a place where family grew instead of a point of conflict that could have started the unraveling of a budding relationship. I don't know what the Filipino leaders told their people on that day, but I suspect that it was fairly similar to what Peter told the faithful about the Gentiles (Acts 15). This church grew because Spirit-led leaders were able to give wise counsel in a difficult time—all of which would not have been successful if the church had not been willing to listen to those Spirit-led leaders.

Solidarity deeply felt and lived out can indeed offer a Christian way of dealing with the issue of ethnic or racial baggage. Such solidarity can lead a community to reconciliation with those feelings, as well as foster willingness to welcome the stranger.

When we are confident that welcoming the other will not undermine who we are, our perception of the other can begin to shift from threat to welcomed addition. Our journey toward a broader sense of self does not push for a redefinition of the self that is diluted or generic. Rather, we have explored our particular sense of self with the intent to clarify the solid foundation that we all have. Such solid grounding can provide the confidence needed to help an individual or group welcome those who are different. This wonderful journey can and does lead us to a place where the stranger is welcomed in expectation of becoming better together instead of fear and worry about losing home.

Notes

1. David Van Biema, "Can Megachurches Bridge the Racial Divide?" *Time*, January 11, 2010.

2. Allan Aubrey Boesak and Curtiss Paul DeYoung, *Radical Reconciliation: Beyond Political Pietism and Christian Quietism* (Maryknoll, NY: Orbis Books, 2012), 70.

3. Miroslav Volf, *Exclusion and Embrace: A Theological Exploration of Identity, Otherness, and Reconciliation* (Nashville: Abingdon, 1996), 101–7.

4. Ibid., 126. Volf here is influenced by Jürgen Moltmann, particularly *The Crucified God* (1972; New York: Harper & Row, 1974); *The Trinity and the Kingdom* (1980; San Francisco: Harper & Row, 1981); *The Way of Jesus Christ* (1989; London: SCM, 1990).

CHAPTER 6

Nurturing Diversity in Community

Now you are the body of Christ, and each one of you
is a part of it. (1 Corinthians 12:27, NIV)

My wife and I recently had our first child. Because we both work, we had to find childcare for him at least twice a week. Conveniently, the church that I serve has an infant room in its daycare. As soon as our son was enrolled, I started to have to maneuver between two roles and two perspectives.

On the one hand, as pastor of the church, I have been uneasy about our entire staff at the daycare and preschool being female. I have often wondered how we could help our school toward gender diversity in its staff. The answer came when a position opened up and one of our best applicants was a man, so we hired him. Then recently we had to let someone go, and again one of the better candidates was a man. We now have two men on staff. As pastor, I was glad that the kids would get to see male teachers as well as female.

On the other hand, I am the father of one of the babies in our daycare. One day I was dropping off our baby at the infant room and was shocked to have a guy—a guy!—take my baby from me for the day. I had pushed for the very thing as a pastor that I was now concerned about as a parent. On that day, when I dropped my son off with a man at daycare for the first time, "we are all equal yet different" took on its full meaning and power. I realized then how my sense of equality had been profoundly skewed by prejudices that I didn't even know I had. That young man had gone through the same background checks and appropriate training for the room that he was to work as had all the other teachers. He, like all the other teachers, was also not allowed ever to be alone with any one child. Yet, knowing all that and having pushed for gender diversity on staff as pastor, I hesitated to entrust my baby to him, a hesitation that would not have been there had the twenty-something young caregiver been a woman.

When was the last time you explored how broad your sense of equality really is? How broad or narrow is that sense in the congregation or group that you are leading? Please take time to explore these questions. I encourage you to write down some examples of how you and your community live and think about equality as you understand it. Add your own stories to the exploration: When did your own difficulty with equality in difference hit you unexpectedly?

Indulge me by allowing me to begin at the beginning. Let us assume that we as individuals and as a congregation are comfortable with keeping equality in diversity separate in our lives. We can assume that we are happy with diversity as a public issue that matters most when we are in public places or at gatherings with people we do not know. As a result, we have been happy to support acceptance of diversity when it is seen as a matter of justice in civic and public life. At the same time, we have kept our understanding of community as a private sphere where our feelings of belonging are more exposed and therefore more at risk. But now we find ourselves at a loss, because a choice that we support in principle from a distance has come to be solidly attached to our church community—a place near us and based on deep connections and exclusivity. Suddenly we find ourselves stuck with a large group of people who should be allowed to move into our home while at the same time we retain our understanding of our home as a limited space.

We need to find ways to redefine the meaning of home, and to find a way to belong again in a manner that includes those we encounter in our journey toward diversity in community. We have to broaden our sense of belonging so that it is no longer limited by our private understanding but instead will help us to live with differences in our midst. In other words, we belong to something greater than ourselves. That something—God-given community— is never something that belongs to us. Becoming free of the need to control a belonging that is ours, we will open a vast space for the other to become community with us. Belonging, then, is no longer separated into a meaningful, private, "we are family" sense and a diluted, public, "we're all human" sense.

For example, how is it that someone whose family has been in Southern California since before the *Mayflower* remains Mexican American while the daughter of a first-generation German immigrant living in San Diego is an all-American California girl? In this example, someone whose roots in California go deep is still considered a foreigner by name because her skin, eye, and hair colors are not of the narrow type needed to belong to the dominant community.

Such a narrow and shallow understanding of community—one that depends on appearances or ethnic background—blocks diversity in our churches. This limited understanding of belonging helps us understand why congregations have so much trouble dealing with diversity that is culturally "foreign."

The problem for our churches is not necessarily diversity in and of itself. After all, we have extensive experience dealing with diversity within our congregations. Every church with more than one individual has to deal with diversity in terms of age, gender, worship tastes, and much more. The difference is that for the majority of our church life we have dealt with diversity as something to be corrected rather than as a desired way of living.

Our job in the church often has been to teach others how to be Christian in the way our particular tradition or congregation has understood that. Diversity in terms of worship styles, doctrinal beliefs, and liturgical practices has been addressed through new-member classes or other strategies to enforce homogeneity for the sake of becoming community. Historically, escaping cultural diversity in Christian community was not difficult because separation (i.e., segregation) was the agreed way to deal with multiculturalism within society at large. To this day most churches still reflect this history of ethnocultural separation. People remember how each ethnicity had its own place, because this was an easy way to be a church. Even our understanding of diversity seems to have been under the yoke of the division between private and public practice. We know how to deal with diversity (by avoiding it or assimilating it) but not how to live with it equally.

Scriptural Definition of Equality

As with most important terms, it is difficult for most of us to agree on exactly what "equality" is. Fortunately, as followers of Christ, we have the guidance of God's word through Scripture. What does the Bible say about equality? In the first part of the fourth chapter of Paul's letter to the churches of Galatia he explains belonging to God by using the illustration of a legal heir, a child positioned to inherit a parent's estate and legacy. This superb illustration concludes by contrasting our former status (as servants or slaves) with our status in Christ (as children and heirs): "So you are no longer a slave but a child, and if a child then also an heir, through God" (Galatians 4:7, NRSV).

God welcomes everyone equally into full status as an heir. Even humans deemed by society to be so insignificant that they could be purchased and sold were welcomed. There are also no geographic limitations on our equality before God: "For my house shall be called a house of prayer for all peoples" (Isaiah 56:7, NRSV [see also Psalm 22:26-28; Isaiah 2:1-3; Acts 17:26-28; 1 Corinthians 1:10-24; Revelation 21:22-26]). What this extremely broad understanding of equality means is further supported by the examples of God's impartial treatment of all.

When Peter found himself in the household of a Roman centurion, he too was hit by how broad God's welcome is. "Then Peter began to speak to them: 'I truly understand that God shows no partiality, but in every nation anyone who fears him and does what is right is acceptable to him'" (Acts 10:34-35, NRSV [see also Romans 2:11; Galatians 2:6; 3:26]). Scripture clearly shows that God does not limit who is to be in intimate community with us.

However, if we limit these passages to a narrow definition, we could still say that while all people can be Christian regardless of ethnicity, social status, and more, we are still free to keep our separations. Nevertheless, God's Word calls for each and every one of us to treat all others as equal children of God. Paul reminds us that we are all "sanctified in Christ Jesus, called to be saints, together with all those who in every place call on the name of our Lord Jesus Christ, both their Lord and ours" (1 Corinthians 1:2, NRSV). The entire Bible, and the New Testament in particular, contains a call of inclusion so encompassing that it requires all of us to see one another as family and to love others as ourselves.

If we still feel that we can make exceptions, Scripture reminds us that there are none in God's call. All the distinctions that create separation between us are shattered by God's call to equality: "There is no longer Jew nor Greek, there is no longer slave or free, there is no longer male or female, for all of you are one in Christ Jesus" (Galatians 3:28, NRSV). There are even stern words for those of us who, after being Christians for a while, may feel knowledgeable enough to discern who is not ready or does not deserve this boundless equality: "My brothers and sisters, do you with your acts of favoritism really believe in our glorious Lord Jesus Christ?" (James

2:1, NRSV [see vv. 1-9]). The limits that create walls between us are devices of our own creation. Our call from God is to *all* so that all people may become heirs of God: "Go therefore and make disciples of all nations" (Matthew 28:18, NRSV).

We must clarify that Scripture does not say that there are no differences among the children of God. Rather, Scripture says that our differences are part of who we are as God's creation. Therefore, because all of us are God's creation, we are also equal though different.

If you are a citizen of or have lived in the United States for a while, you know that talk of equality is everywhere, and for the most part all of us are good at saying the right things in the right way. We are constantly reminded of the immigrant roots of our country. Saint Patrick's Day and Cinco de Mayo, lasagna and gyros, polkas and reggae—these and many more offer clear yet often overlooked reminders of immigrants' attempts to retain a piece of their previous homes while shaping a new home in the United States of America. Many of our local churches themselves were immigrant enclaves in origin.[1] The town of Bridgeport, Pennsylvania, exemplifies this enclave approach. This small town

Scriptural Descriptions of Equality

Believers go from slave to child of God, and therefore are an heir. (Galatians 4:7)

Believers come from all nations. (Jeremiah 31:8; Acts 10:34-35)

Believers are called to be holy people. (1 Corinthians 1:2)

All are one in Jesus Christ; there are no distinctions of ethnicity, gender, or social status. (Galatians 3:28)

Each member of the body has value; all function together. (1 Corinthians 12)

Favoritism has no place among those who believe in Jesus. (James 2:1)

had several Catholic churches because each ethnic group needed to worship separately. This separation goes as far back as our origins in the colonies. "*Mary*land" founding as a haven for catholics is probably one of the most obvious in name. Yet, the way we understand that history seems to be compartmentalized in such a way as to ensure separation. It seems that we have grown to see cultural diversity as a plus in the open popular spaces but a threat in the private groups that feed our sense of belonging.

This dialectic understanding of diversity and the resulting difficulties are clearly shown in the history of our country and churches. We bled to do away with slavery in the nineteenth century, yet soon after we developed a system that kept the extreme structural inequality going well into the twentieth century. The church does not escape fault. Many churches have clamored for the poor and destitute at an emotional level but at the same time have been unable or unwilling to welcome them in their own homes, thus forcing them into their own ethnic churches.[2] Many of us have come to feel encouraged by and even proud of ethnic diversity in our denominations while at the same making sure that our own congregation does not change. These difficulties are the inevitable side effects of a narrow, shallow understanding of an equality that could exist in segregation. (Remember the fallacy of "separate but equal"?)

Equality in Diversity

We have now arrived at an important place in our pilgrimage. At this stage of the journey many people begin to doubt and some give up. Though we are not too far along, we can see that the trip is going to be more difficult than we anticipated. Anyone who gives you ten easy steps to multicultural Christian community is glossing over much of the pain and work. But let us not be discouraged. We have been walking an uphill path, but at the end is a vantage point from which we can see more of the context of our difficult road.

Equality and Diversity Have Power

From our vantage point we can see the power and volatility of the mixture of equality and diversity. These two powerful forces are not mixed often. As we have noted in previous chapters, diversity is difficult when we have the best of intentions and desires. So, when we mix diversity into an existing church, or worse yet, one in danger of closing, we end up with a powder keg that can explode at any minute. As a result, the choices that we make can have long-lasting consequences for our community.

That powder keg forces us into making choices about how to deal with that powerful force. The first choice is how we view this powder keg. We can look at its potential for destruction and do our best to contain it, by giving it a wide berth or by putting it away as far out of sight as we can. Or, we can perceive its potential for transformation, and then put on our grace gloves, keep water close by, and set about the work of making productive use of its explosive energy. At the center of the difficulty is the fact that equality and diversity are often put together as words, but we have little experience living with this situation. The gap between saying and doing is much wider than we would like to admit to ourselves.

At a conference where I spoke on diversity, a man approached me to chat about Guatemala because I had mentioned that I was born there. His demeanor let me know that he truly felt called to serve in Guatemala. His words showed me that there had been no death of his ego, and therefore he had a passion for diversity but not a hint of equality. Many of his sentences started in the following ways: "These poor people"; "If they would only see what they're doing wrong"; "I should know; I've been there every year the last ten years"; "What they need to do is. . . ." On and on he went, talking to a Guatemalan as if he were an expert on his interlocutor's country after having been there a total of ten to fifteen weeks in the course of a decade. Nothing about the way he delivered his pronouncements betrayed any sign of an inflated sense of worth. He seemed to believe what he was saying, including the fact that he was an expert on my country.

As you can imagine, I was not a happy person during my conversation with this man. When I mentioned to him how it might be difficult to be an expert about a country after less than four months total in it, he disagreed because he thought his methodology to be sound, and as an outsider he had greater perspective. How would you feel if a Guatemalan who spoke little to no English gave you a rundown of the United States after spending a total of one summer in it, justifying the comments by claiming to be an expert about your country? Does the powder keg need the water you were keeping next to it?

Diversity on its own is difficult, and in order for it to become part of life in our community, we must include equality in the equation. If we want equality to work, we must have a deep exploration of the self as well as the courage to know that often this journey leads to the death of the old self to make room for the new, loving community. Otherwise the powder keg will explode, and we will hurt ourselves and others in the process.

Ambiguity in the Life of the Church

As a guest speaker at a church, I told stories of how someone who looks like me, a Latino man, lives with subtle and sometimes obvious prejudicial treatment. I saw how upset those in attendance were on my behalf when I told them the stories. After the event ended, there was time for fellowship. Two women came up to me, and we started chatting about various things. Then we came to chatting about the examples that I had mentioned. One woman said, "We talked, and we think that you don't look Latino enough to have that much trouble."

I love this comment because it illustrates the ambiguity with which many of us at church live. Everyone recognizes that there is a problem that needs to be addressed, and we have a deeply felt reaction against the situation still existing (i.e., Latinos often are perceived in a negative, prejudiced way). At the same time, we also accept and recognize that there is a type of person who is often free of troubles based on appearance alone: "We think that you don't look Latino enough. . . ." Being light-skinned is considered a great advantage in just about all communities of color. We all live in this ambiguity, and we all allow it to be perpetuated.

The unspoken rule that dictates that the lighter a person is, the easier life becomes, affects the process of moving into diversity in community. If the prejudices that come from thinking that skin tone determines how nice, responsible, and productive a person is are left unexplored, they could derail the process toward equality in diversity. That need of exploration is why we have not considered diversity in community until this chapter. The previous chapter was part of the preparation for this journey. The intent to broaden our sense of self makes more space for community with those different from us. We need to make room for differences in order to consider how to live with others in the intimacy of our chosen groups. So, how do we work our way from wherever we are in our journey to diversity in community as the destination shown to us throughout Scripture?

Equality in the Midst of Differences

Perhaps the expression "we are all equal yet different" can help us to open our private selves and communal spaces. As we look at our community more closely, we may notice that we have placed *equality* and *similarity* so close to each other in meaning that they are nearly indistinguishable. In other words, we want people who are equal to each other to also be similar in exterior ways, ethnicity, socioeconomic status, education level, etc. So, "we are all equal yet different" points us in the right direction, but only insofar as a compass can point us to our destination.

"Equality in the midst of difference" gives us a direction in which to travel. What we need next is a clearly marked path that carries us toward that elusive life of equality in diversity. One such path is life in solidarity. Recall that living in solidarity means that we become ever more important parts of one another's lives as we walk together, risk together, and suffer together. Therefore, the path of solidarity that we take as individuals eventually can lead our community to equality. In fact, once we have walked the path of solidarity for a while, we are afforded a closer and clearer look at equality.

As we reach the vantage point achieved through solidarity, it will become easier to notice wonderfully freeing aspects of equality. For one, equality does not have to mean sameness. Walking in this close way creates intimacy, which in turn opens room for love to grow. To walk in solidarity rooted in love does not require either side to become the other. In fact, it is the differences between those walking together that help them along. Love then expands our sense of belonging in such a way that our differences change from difficulties with which to contend into assets to use in our journey.

Walking in solidarity we can see how our differences strengthen our community. When our strength comes from our diversity, we no longer all try to be the best at one thing. Instead, we all share in the benefits of different skill sets. Following the path of solidarity as a community leads us to sharing the differences among ourselves for the benefit of all. Solidarity shows that something can be greater than the sum of its parts.

Years ago our church started class in English as a second language (ESL). The beginning of that class was one of the most wonderful beginnings I have had the joy of experiencing. We had the support of the congregation, both emotional as well as material in the form of physical space and financial resources. We had two bilingual teachers who had spent time in the very countries of the Latinos who were the majority of those in need of learning English.

The program that we created was tailored for the community in which we lived. All in all, I felt that we had as good a chance of success as can be had. We advertised by print and word of mouth and had a number of people who seemed interested. The first day of class came, and we had two teachers and one student.

Having only one student was not a problem because we knew that the program was just starting. I did not start to worry until, at three months, we had at most three students in any given class. What was worse, it was not even the same three students. People in the neighborhood knew about the class and seemed to enjoy it while they were there, but for some reason they were not coming regularly, or at all. So I reviewed our curriculum and talked to people in the community about what they needed from ESL classes to make sure that we were providing it. I also asked the students themselves about our teaching styles and the pace to see if too much information too quickly was the problem. Nothing seemed to be wrong.

After about four months a young woman came who liked to talk. She came back the next week, and for the several weeks that followed we found ourselves starting class late because she would catch us up on her week, ask us and whoever else was there about our week, and listen like it mattered. Soon the class started to grow, and as it did, the reason became as obvious to us as I am sure it is to you. The class was fine for what it was, but it had offered no personal connections. I was so busy trying to give people the education that I thought they needed that I hadn't asked them if ESL was *all* they needed. They didn't want a community based only in information/content; they needed a community of solidarity, one that would walk alongside them.

The Imagery of the Body

Now that we have a direction and a path to take, we may still need to clarify what equality means in the mess diversity brings. The apostle Paul took the gospel to the Gentile world, and many of the churches to which he was writing in his epistles were in culturally and ethnically diverse cosmopolitan places. His létters illustrate how something can be greater than the sum of its parts. For example, let us look at a verse from Paul's first letter to the Corinthians: "The eye cannot say to the hand, 'I have no need of you,' nor again the head to the feet, 'I have no need of you'" (1 Corinthians 12:21, NRSV). In this metaphor of the human body, we find disparate body parts saying that they do not need each other. We may miss the power of this analogy because, although we all have bodies, we rarely have the opportunity to see the incredible complexity involved in getting all the parts to work together in a useful way. Often people who have recovered sight after being blind since birth or early childhood prefer to keep their eyes closed to engage with the world around them.[3] It may take these people months to identify objects or recognize faces. In the midst of the difficulty of having received a gift that most people think is wonderful, these people are tempted to say, "I do not need you, eye." So, however great those of us with sight may feel that it would be for a blind person to see, unless we walk with that person, we cannot know the challenges presented by this enormous transition from blindness to sight.

The power of the imagery of the body can only be as strong, fulfilling, and supportive as we are willing to embrace. Paul intended the body metaphor to explain life in Christian community. Mutual need arising from valuing diversity helps us move on the path toward equality. An understanding of living together in solidarity is a fundamental aspect of traveling to diversity in community.

Notes

1. Charles P. Lutz, *Church Roots: Stories of Nine Immigrant Groups That Became the American Lutheran Church* (Minneapolis: Augsburg, 1985).

2. Michael O. Emerson and Christian Smith, *Divided by Faith: Evangelical Religion and the Problem of Race in America* (Oxford: Oxford University Press, 2000), 21–50.

3. Robert Kurson, *Crashing Through: The Extraordinary True Story of the Man Who Dared to See* (New York: Random House, 2008).

CHAPTER 7

Walking in Solidarity

For as in one body we have many members, and not
all the members have the same function, so we, who
are many, are one body in Christ, and individually we
are members one of another. (Romans 12:4-5, NRSV)

Knowing the direction and having identified the path to our destination does not guarantee our completion of the journey. As we
move further along the road of solidarity to equality, some baggage
we may still be carrying from our pre-journey world could become
increasingly apparent. We might begin to notice even more clearly
how life in need of each other, in solidarity, goes against many of
the things held dearly in our culture and praised in our media outlets. Our culture prizes the glorious day when any one of us can
say, "I do not need anyone!" For example, one of the first things
that the media let us know about a lottery winner is how he told
his boss that he is not coming back to work. As the woman
recounts that story, we can see the glee in her eye—as if working
was exclusively for people who have no other option.

Yet, not only does Scripture tell us we cannot live without each
other, but also it says that this must be without exception: "The eye
cannot say to the hand, 'I have no need of you'" (1 Corinthians
12:21). It is difficult to imagine two things more different in form
and function than an eye and a hand, yet as parts of the body, nei-

ther can tell the other that it is not needed. After all, the body would suffer greatly by the loss of either of those two parts. Walking in solidarity opens the door for others to become people who matter to us, and thus allows us to see through the dense and blinding foliage of our culture and our prejudices. Our journey into diversity in community has already been long, but we have just arrived at equality. We have yet to experience it.

Equality Rooted in Love

We will know that we are experiencing equality when belonging has permeated our multicultural relationships. In chapter 5 we looked at belonging as the vehicle that took us to a deeper understanding of ourselves. That particular stage of our journey came with the added benefit of recognizing that our identity does not need to be diluted or surrendered when we move toward diversity. Instead, a broader and deeper sense of self allows us to make room for those different from us so that neither loses oneself in the other. This view lets us know that we are not going to run out of space or pieces of the pie. The room that we discover together is one that does not take away from any of us; it builds and helps us all.

Chapter 5's short hike into exploring belonging and the self ultimately led us to Miroslav Volf's archetypes and the road that takes us toward solidarity. As we walked that path, we came to see the need for sharing with one another long enough for the relationship to grow roots of love, which in turn grow equality.

A deep sense of equality rooted in love is what we call living in solidarity. The longer we spend on the road to solidarity, the easier it becomes to encounter the other with a sense of equality and even expectation of a hoped-for mutual benefit from the encounter. As we continue journeying in solidarity with the other, their world begins to affect us because our worlds are combining. In turn, new worlds are birthed, and from them our own home looks different.

These new worlds are difficult and incredibly rewarding at the same time. We find ourselves suffering with those who are unjustly treated in ways that affect us intimately. We also find ourselves enriched by the abundance of life that those different from us bring. In essence, solidarity brings us to the sense of community described in Hebrews 13:3: "Remember those who are in prison, as though you were in prison with them; those who are being tortured, as though you yourselves were being tortured" (NRSV).

Another aspect of equality through solidarity is that it moves us beyond our current faith world. A new faith world is opened when solidarity takes hold of us and settles in. We begin to see that "we" are trapped in the same boat with "them." Curiously, as the distance from the other shrinks to adjust to the new, cramped reality that we are discovering, the borders of our faith and the boundaries of our home begin to expand. This shrinking of space between us and our neighbors expands our sense of home, and our faith relationship begins to include more than God and ourselves. In other words, a personal relationship with Jesus Christ comes to its proper place as the beginning of a journey, not the destination.

Soon enough our relationships with God, self, and our church begin to be challenged as our new reality takes hold. We find greater perspective as we travel further away from the old, small world in which we lived. When we have traveled a good distance into this new and life-giving faith world, we can look back and see how small our faith country had been.

Take a moment and think about the important matters in your life during childhood. Recall how your best friend sat next to someone else that long-ago day in the bus, or that one Christmas when you did not get the exact toy you wanted. How important were those things when you reached high school, or started college, or entered the job market? In a similar way, growth that comes from a spiritual journey to equality changes one's perception of the difficulty of a challenging situation. Difficulties that seemed near impossibilities at the beginning can become little more than a memory that reminds us of who we were but do not challenge us in the same way. Distance gained by walking the path of solidarity gives us a greater vantage point as we go further into the journey. That greater distance also leads us to see clearly that the journey that we have undertaken is about much more than one's faith and local church. We are not moving toward a multicultural Christian community only because we are called to show people that they need Jesus or because it will help keep our church stay open. Rather, we are called into a richly multicultural life because that is the life that Jesus wants for us all.

So, the journey toward diversity in community is about those beyond our borders, but in a different way than we may want. We may have started our journey as though it were a business trip where we went to a foreign land to let the people there know why they need what we have. But in solidarity we learned that we are in just as much need as those beyond our walls. We realize more deeply that the mutual need is not a pain-free experience; it is often a trip that is uphill and on rocky or sandy ground.

The apostle Paul wrote, "I appeal to you therefore, brothers and sisters, by the mercies of God, to present your bodies as a living sacrifice, holy and acceptable to God" (Romans 12:1, NRSV). The problem, of course, continues to be the distance between saying and doing. I wonder how many of us have read and heard these words from Romans and felt the deep emotional desire to present ourselves to God in just such a way. The difficulty centers on making sure that we hear these words as Paul intended. In his time and place, a living sacrifice did not mean giving up chocolate for forty days. It never went well for the longevity of the life that was sacrificed. So, in a profound and uncomfortable way, there is no escaping the necessary death that must take place, "for those who want to save their life will lose it" (Luke 9:24, NRSV)—and not only their life, but also their church.

Our history as a nation and the demographics of our churches tell us that when it comes to welcoming those who are different, many walls need to be torn down. These are not merely physical walls in the churchyard. These walls are close in, precious to us, ones that we have come to love and feel protected by. God does indeed call us to sacrifice far more than our comforts. "You shall love your neighbor as yourself" (Matthew 22:39, NRSV) makes clear the need for sacrifice in our faith lives.

Equality Stabilizes Diversity

It would be good for us to revisit Miroslav Volf's categories for engaging with the other. Recall that his book *Exclusion and Embrace* offers three approaches to deal with the combination of diversity and equality: universal, communitarian, and postmodern.[1] All of these options take as their premise the need to find a place for our differences. None of these approaches engage with the differences in a nuanced way with the intent of living with those differences. Rather, the strategies aim to create a safe place in which to store the differences. In other words, one way to deal with this volatile mixture is to contain it, put a large sign on it that says "Keep Out," and avoid that space.

Equality can come into this space and disrupt our commonly used strategies by placing love as the ingredient that transforms the volatile mixture into a stable compound. Diversity keeps its explosive power, yet equality makes it safe enough to handle and to use constructively.

During the 1800s, everyone was aware of the raw power of nitroglycerin as an explosive. It was highly valued, but its volatility detracted from how and where it could be used. By contrast, trinitrotoluene (more familiarly known as TNT) is so stable that it went years without being classified as an explosive. It took years of patience, curiosity, and research for people to learn how to release the power of TNT.[2] Many of our congregations look for a spiritual nitroglycerin that will deliver quick results and change their churches into a megachurch in a couple of years. At the same time, they ignore the components of the TNT they already have that can serve just as well but in a safer and more productive way.

TNT and nitroglycerin are two very different substances used for very similar purposes. Nitroglycerin was obvious and dangerous, but everyone knew that it explodes. Church growth materials from churches that experienced explosive growth are obvious examples of "success," and everyone has seen the explosion. TNT, on the other hand, for many years was not even identified as something that could explode. Similarly, many of our dying churches have spent resources for years looking for the right kind of nitroglycerin while their own TNT goes unused.

Worry can make churches look for that quick, explosive solution. The problem is that these dying-to-megachurch-in-ten-steps solutions, like nitroglycerin, are too often as destructive as they are helpful. A pastor in California used one of these approaches when he joined a group called G12. The purpose of this group is quick, explosive growth through a small-group pyramid scheme. (You can learn more about it online with a basic Google search.) But because the group demands complete allegiance from its members and strict adherence to its methods, it functions more like a cult than a community of faith. The pastor seeking to grow his church through G12 saw the effort implode. "When we decided to do G12, I was left with eight people at the church," the pastor admitted. Feeling betrayed by the manipulations of G12's strategies, formerly loyal church members abandoned the congregation, destroying the church.

Measuring Equality

So, how does equality stabilize diversity in community in such a way as to keep the explosive power while canceling the volatility? First, it lets us know when we are settling for a marginal diversity.

Simply having people of different cultures in the same place is a difficult task for many groups, including churches. Often the work is so exhausting that groups declare victory and never move beyond a state of pseudo-diversity that is void of equality. That environment will lead to discontent from the bottom and frustration from the top. To stop here is tantamount to ending our journey while having barely left the borders of our own town. We can see in the story that follows how arriving at our border and calling that Samaria does not get us beyond our world as Jesus intends by calling us to go to Samaria.

There are wonderful congregations that have welcomed and aided immigrant or refugee families until they can get on their feet; then the church seems to assume that these guests can be on their way. Often the immigrants want to stay, but they have been given only space without equality. I once visited a church that had a strong refugee group that even had its own worship time on Sunday afternoons. That community was growing and rivaling the "real" service in numbers and activity. But the congregation itself, during its regular life, still looked like it always had, and the pool for leadership remained what it had always been. This church had diversity but not equality. The result was that the families that wanted to stay because they were welcomed by this church started moving away.

Other congregations take pride in how many countries are represented at worship but rarely go beyond hanging flags of various nations or having an international festival with different foods being served. Since settling is so very tempting, it is important to assess the community for its practice of equality because that helps the leader gauge how the congregation is doing in its journey toward diversity in community.

There are many ways to measure equality in the midst of diversity. You as the leader could arrange your measuring instrument in two broad categories: leadership and community.

Leadership. To what extent do your worship services reflect diversity in leadership? Whom does the congregation see up front, in charge of events, reading Scripture, organizing events, leading worship, chairing committees, and more? How about diversity on your pastoral staff and church committees, boards, and ministry teams? To what degree are the voices and opinions of new members taken into account regarding important choices for the church?

Community. How often do groups within your congregation spend time together? What fellowship opportunities allow people to interact across generations, cultures, and life experience? Are your small groups diverse? Do various age, ethnic, and cultural groups spend time together socially?

Some congregations will say, "We may not be ethnically diverse, but there are plenty of youth or older members in our church." Again the question is this: What voice do these diverse groups have in the choice-making of the church? Diversity is not limited to the ethnic or cultural variety. Equality still needs to be an integral part of any diversity in order to continue the journey toward Christian multiculturalism.

The church leader needs to know that stepping into diversity is difficult; there is constant pressure to end up settling in before the journey gets going. Yet, it is precisely in that difficult place where equality reminds us that things need to be much deeper. When we include equal love in our relationships, love asks why we are keeping people out of choosing our shared life and future together. It is not enough for those in leadership to be aware that we need to listen to all. Equal love also demands that authority be shared so thoroughly that we all have to listen to one another in order to decide our future together.

Gaining a Different Perspective

Second, equality helps our heart join in the journey. The church that I serve is located in a state where the legislature was considering a draconian immigration law. One of our church members came to me to ask about the proposed measures. After some chatting, the conversation came down to a measure that would prohibit the transportation of undocumented immigrants in any vehicle. The parishioner suddenly asked, "Wait, does this mean I can get in trouble if I'm pulled over and Maria [not her real name] is with me in the car?" I said, "Yes, and you can get anything from a ticket to your car being impounded." I noticed the parishioner's facial expressions turn from curiosity to near anger as the parishioner went on to say, "That's just stupid. I hope it doesn't pass."[3]

Walking in solidarity helps our heart enter into another person's world. Then we get an entirely different perspective, and what we once thought was clear turns out to be murky and clouded. The deeper our relationship with another gets, the easier it becomes to come to an awareness of the other's needs. The desire to help and be supportive grows because when we know and care for someone, that person's needs and preferences become important. So, as love enters into the mixture between diversity and equality, many of our differences change from seeming threatening and unwanted to important and necessary for the sake of those we love.

Maneuvering through Difficulties

Third, equality supports us all through the difficulties that will come. We all know that hard times will come and go throughout every person's life. But it is good to know that the way we maneuver through these difficulties is greatly supported by the love we receive from those around us. Because this love is mutual and deep, it helps us persevere through ongoing difficulties. As Paul says, "We also rejoice in our sufferings, knowing that suffering produces endurance, and endurance produces character, and character produces hope, and hope does not disappoint us, because God's love has been poured into our hearts through the Holy Spirit which has been given to us" (Romans 5:3-5, RSV).

During the late 1970s into 1983 in Argentina, there was what came to be known as the Dirty War. During that time people simply disappeared. In 1977, fourteen mothers came to the most important plaza in Argentina, Plaza de Mayo, to ask the military government for information regarding their children. A movement was born out of that protest that is active to this day. Many in that group have spent decades in search of family members, as well as the children of their sisters and brothers in solidarity. These women and their families have lived through unthinkable difficulties. Yet, for decades the equality that resulted from the love that grew out of walking in solidarity has sustained them in their seemingly impossible task.

The journey toward diversity in equality is not short, nor is it easy. However, by having love seep into this mixture by way of growing equality among us and our neighbors, we can develop the perseverance that we need to disrupt our inadequate patterns into a new way of living and loving. The volatile mixture of diversity in community can be stabilized by the equality that love brings. The new mixture is powerful, yet very stable. It can be wielded to fuel the continued journey into new life in our communities of faith. In other words, equality rooted in love can move diversity in community out of our event posters, praise and worship songs, inclusive prayers, and visioning sessions into a walked and lived reality. With equality rooted in love, we can add walking the walk to the talking that we do.

Creating a New Home

A fourth way that equality in community can help is that it moves us beyond the comfortable compounds that we are tempted to create when we leave home. During the golden era of our missionary work, we sent large numbers of missionaries to live in exotic countries. Many of our missionaries carved out little pieces of home that came to be called compounds—communities made up of people like them from which they would go out and make disciples in their own image. The result was that we created disciples of Western European Christianity. To this day, there are places in Asia and Latin America where the US pre-1950s worship style is alive and well.

Of course, it would be unfair and anachronistic to judge those missionaries through the lenses of our current multicultural and pluralistic society. However, this illustration serves to remind us that when it comes to moving toward fully inclusive diversity, we are indeed in a different world. We are traveling into the mission field around us because God calls us to share the love that we have received with the world as neighbors in equality.

In order to share the love of God as we have been commanded, we must do so in the way we have received it: freely and indiscriminately. Diversity in community can help us travel into the world and share in God's love equally.

When we find ourselves living in equality with our neighbors, we experience their world in a profound and moving way. We can also look back and see our own world from an entirely different perspective. Being out in the field and exposed to the world with the other is a powerful tool to move us to profound equality. In the intimate community that is created in solidarity, we are all transformed thoroughly, from the core of our own identities to the words and deeds that we give the world.

Notes

1. Miroslav Volf, *Exclusion and Embrace: A Theological Exploration of Identity, Otherness, and Reconciliation* (Nashville: Abingdon, 1996), 101–7.

2. G. I. Brown, *The Big Bang: A History of Explosives* (Stroud: Sutton Publishing, 1998), 151–53.

3. A note of caution: I am aware that we are not all in agreement with regard to this issue. This anecdote is from one person's point of view.

CHAPTER 8

Walking through Samaria

[Jesus asked,] "Which of these three, do you think,
was a neighbor to the man who fell into the hands of
robbers?" He [the expert in the law] said, "The one
who showed him mercy." Jesus said to him, "Go and
do likewise." (Luke 10:36-37, NRSV)

The Jews of Jesus' time had serious problems with Samaritans and
vice versa. Such was their mutual animosity that they would avoid
each other even to the point of uncomfortable inconvenience. "A
few years before Jesus told this parable, some Samaritans took
their pack animals into the holy places of Judaism and let them
defecate there to show their disdain for Jewish religion, so
Samaritans were viewed as blasphemers."[1] No Jew would set foot
in Samaria unless it was unavoidable. However, it is clear that Jesus
led his disciples and other Jews directly into Samaria several times.

Why would Jesus use the imagery of Samaria with those he was
leading toward change? Jesus was showing his followers the good
in the worst type of people they could imagine. He wanted the Jews
not only to think about Samaria but also to walk through it.

In 2005, Morgan Spurlock began a reality television program
called *30 Days*. The premise of the show was to have a person
spend a month with people who were vastly different from that
person. One episode had a Minute Man, who watched the border

with Mexico to make sure that no one crossed into the United States, live with an undocumented family for thirty days. The reason Jesus had a Samaritan be the good guy in the parable was precisely to move his Jewish listeners past their firm and faithfully held borders. The best way to help people see what is on the other side is to take them there.

Why Walk through Samaria?

Understanding the shock value and negative connotation of Samaria in Scripture isn't easy for us to grasp today. Our current world surrounds us with signs telling us that being a Samaritan is good. In fact, most of the time when we hear the word "Samaritan," it is preceded by the word "good." However, the way we see Samaritans now has more to do with what we as the church have done with the biblical parable of the good Samaritan than with the historical reality of why Jesus chose a Samaritan to be the character who was "good." When we read the Gospels in context, we see how offensive it was for Jesus to use a Samaritan as an example of goodness, above even the holy men of Israel. We are far away from the emotions that Jesus wanted to elicit by using Samaritans in his parable and in his travels with his disciples. Therefore, we have to work harder at experiencing the intended emotional journey from these encounters to see the profound relevance of Samaritans to our journey into Christian multiculturalism.

What sort of feelings did Jesus want to elicit from his fellow Jews by using a Samaritan as an example of good? I think that Jesus wanted us to feel love that is able to reach even as far as those we despise. Understandably, Samaria does not hold the same power to offend for us as it did for the Jews listening to Jesus. Fortunately, there is something fairly simple that we can do to experience those feelings here and now.

In order to explore these feelings, we need only to do two mental exercises. First, think of a type of person or an ethnicity that elicits anger in you. It is important that your reaction be raw and intense. It must be someone or a group of people who may have even desecrated what you hold sacred. Who is it? Whose presence would make your blood boil?

Second, think of a place or country that you would never want to visit because it seems horrible. Why that place is horrible is up to you. It would be best if it is somewhere you know you are not welcome, and you probably also know that the feeling is mutual. Now, I'm sure you know that I will ask you to place the names you just identified in the stories of Samaritan encounters with Jesus. If you have been honest with yourself, then "the parable of the good _____" (fill in the blank) should now be offensive to you, or at the least make you want to ask Jesus why he chose such a horrible person.

Still, why would Jesus want the Jews to go through the discomfort of walking physically (John 4) and spiritually (Luke 10) in Samaria? We know that Jesus' actions were always purposeful, so it is safe to assume that Jesus did not use a Samaritan in his parable simply to get a rise out of the Jews who were listening. Jesus also did not speak to a woman alone simply to shock his disciples. Therefore, given what we know of Jesus, he must have intended these situations to be helpful to those experiencing them, then and since.

When Jesus took his disciples into Samaria, he was not just intending to show them how the other side lives. The reason Jesus was alone with the woman at the well (John 4) was that the disciples had gone to a Samaritan town to buy food. This was a full-immersion journey. Not only was Jesus having these Jews travel into Samaria, but also they had to get their nourishment from people they were taught to hate. Further, by engaging the Samaritan woman, Jesus was modeling for his community how to begin the process to see life from within, to commune with "them." When the woman returned to town, her fellow Samaritans had already shared food with Jews.

I see two reasons why this story can help us move into a new place as a community.

First, there is no better way to see the world from a different perspective than to walk in someone else's shoes for a while. Walking in someone else's shoes puts congregations in a difficult spot because most of us are not in the places of those we wish to help. For many churches, the poor, dispossessed, or alien are little more than words and perhaps pictures we have seen on television or for a week during our mission trips. But the fear, anxiety, or even disgust that we have toward those strangers who need help are felt in real ways. Perhaps the following event will help illustrate this point.

There is a program in Philadelphia in which churches on the periphery of the city take turns being an overnight shelter for the homeless. The program would take care of everything; all the church had to do was provide space. The homeless would be brought to the church, supervised by staff, and brought back to the city in the morning. In the mid 2000s one church from a wealthy suburb decided to join the program, as they had plenty of space and wanted to help. People in town quickly found out what was happening, and within a day flyers were distributed to all in the neighborhood:

> Would you like to have possible criminals walking our streets and living among us?
>   Say no to homeless in our backyards, call [the church], and tell them to say no!

The church decided to withdraw from the program. Instead, they donated the funds to help other churches pay for expenses such as heat, food, and other things. I didn't know the church very well, but I've always wondered what took place during the discussions that led to withdrawing from that program. Was a church member the author of the flyer? Did the congregation discuss the obvious lies and exaggerations in that flyer? Did donors threaten to withdraw their money? Most worrisome still, why did this community give up the chance to follow Jesus into Samaria? They gave up on a chance to see the other, the Samaritans, as people. The layers of statistics, assumptions, prejudices, and ignorance could have been washed away one by one by the pressure washer of close personal interactions. Sadly, the church closed in and went back to being a refuge from the world instead of a safe haven for the suffering of the world.

A church in a journey toward Christian diversity must spend time in Samaria. It needs to find itself exposed to its own fears and those of the world around it. Sending funds is very helpful but does very little for the church's journey. When we have seen and experienced life with the "least of these," it becomes more difficult to retain our prejudices and fears. When we have lived with outsiders, general terms about them become more difficult to accept. "They are all lazy" is much more difficult to accept when one has seen one of "them" wake up before dawn to work from 7 a.m. to 7 p.m. six days a week. It is much more difficult to accept that "most poor people are poor because they have no motivation to change their circumstances" when one has spent time with a nine-year-old child who is left at home with hot dogs, buns, and a pot full of water on the stove because mom is at work and dad is long gone. Her minimum-wage check is exhausted on rent and heat, and there is more than a week left until the next check. The child did not create these circumstances, and yet many still hold the child responsible. How can this child get the help that is badly needed?

Of course, the problem with learning these lessons from Samaria is that one has to go there and stay for a while. In the time of Jesus, when walking was the main mode of transportation, it was common to have to spend a considerable amount of time in or near a particular place. Our current world has transportation and other means that make it easy to live near the poor or the other without ever seeing them. We have forgotten what it is like to walk everywhere. Could you imagine having to walk to work? Or when visiting relatives in other states, walking to see them? Walking somewhere is a slow process in which we cannot escape relationship with those in places where we walk and rest. So it is with spending time with those whom we mean to help. If we walk with the other as Jesus calls us to, we should not be able to escape relationship with them.

Yet, how are we to learn from a Samaria that we never visit? For most of us, our Samaria is not far away. I would even risk saying that the majority of churches that are suffering with fewer people and may even be at risk of closing are located in the Samaria to which Jesus is calling them. So, the beginning of the solution can be as simple and as complicated as stepping outside the church and asking, "Whom do I know in this town, city, area?" Notice the difference between "whom do I know?" and "who knows us?" Most church growth programs want to help you get people to know who you are. That presumes that we are what people need.

Of course, this sojourn in Samaria will involve both sides of that relational dynamic, but if we do not begin with figuring out those whom we know, it will be difficult to know if we have what people need. For a leader, that seemingly simple task can take much effort to accomplish. Jesus had to break with convention and risk disapproval in the process. Jesus talked to a woman who was by herself and a Samaritan (John 4:7-26). In that encounter, when Jesus took a risk, an entire town was changed. Of course, neither you nor I, nor our church, is Jesus. But the least we can do is take a risk and talk to the people in the Samarias that surround us.

Because we have agreed to this trip and are well on our way, from now on our conversation will be from within the foreign land to which we have been traveling.

As we have known from the beginning, this new land is different and therefore uncomfortable and strange at times. This new land is most certainly not home. In fact, many of us have been looking across at the strange new world with concern and even dread for a long time, and crossing the border into it sometimes makes things worse at first.

Paradoxically, few things are different about this new world because it is still the physical world in which we have been living for a long time. Most things will look the same. Our church building will remain where it is. The way we get to our church will still be the familiar route. But if we have undertaken the exploration leading to this point, our familiar world may also feel small and even insufficiently inhabited in important ways. This change of view does not necessarily mean that we have changed who we are. But who we are has grown in depth as well as perspective. After all, traveling does tend to broaden one's horizons, particularly in the intentional way we are engaging in our journey toward Christian diversity. It is understandable that where we were prior to the beginning of our journey may feel small when we look back.

As we look back across the border to our home, let us begin by recognizing the common experience of perceiving home as smaller than we remembered after significant travel. Also, let us take courage and inspiration by remembering that we are not the only ones to have had to undertake a journey into the unknown for the sake of our faith. In Scripture we find many people traveling to the unknown.

The Search for a Scapegoat

The Israelites said to them, "If only we had died by the hand of the LORD in Egypt, when we sat by the fleshpots and ate our fill of bread; for you have brought us out into this wilderness to kill this whole assembly with hunger." (Exodus 16:3, NRSV)

Moving into new territory is difficult. Encouraging others to do the same can feel almost impossible to a leader. Still, I would like to highlight another important aspect of the power that places like Samaria have over us. When we are in our journey in Samaria and something goes wrong, it is nearly impossible for most of us to look at ourselves when looking to place blame. When something goes wrong in a church, it often takes a miracle to help that church look at itself as a possible cause for the problems. The reasons for our difficulty to see how we contribute to our own trouble are complicated, yet we can begin this section of our journey by taking two paths, the first leading to the second.

The first is to acknowledge how little information we need to confirm our prejudices. An important aspect of this path is how our remarkable ability to travel exposes us to differences just long enough to create prejudices or have them confirmed by a cursory view that is colored by our prejudgments. Have you ever found yourself lost in a bad part of town? How many of the young men you saw there looked suspicious to you? Is it really the case that all those young men were looking for trouble? What you were seeing has come to be known as confirmation bias. "Your opinions are the result of years of paying attention to information that confirmed what you believed, while ignoring information that challenged your preconceived notions."[2]

When we find ourselves in a Samaria, what we see is not entirely what we are looking at. Therefore, because we tend to see and interpret according to our confirmation bias, it becomes difficult to live in Samaria. What is worse, when trouble comes, our biased view can make a difficulty be perceived as a full-blown crisis. Then, when we are in crisis, it becomes even more difficult to see clearly. Therefore, these perceptions make it much easier to look for who is at fault than to explore our own contribution to what is going on. Conveniently for our ego, our brief interactions, as well as the media that we choose to watch or read, offer plenty of scapegoat material. Who is your church blaming for its difficulties?

Our search for someone or something to blame during difficulties thus takes us to the second path in our exploration of life in our Samaria. The second is what the theologian René Girard calls the scapegoat theory. Girard deals with our tendency toward scapegoating in depth in his book *I See Satan Fall Like Lightning*.[3] In essence, the concept of scapegoating is that we as individuals and as a community tend to look for someone to blame during difficult times, and that scapegoat is generally the group or person we like the least.

I was recently involved in a Facebook discussion on the issue of gun regulation. As the discussion developed, I noticed how everyone was busy blaming the opposing side for the problem while at the same time explaining how if people would only listen to their side, this complicated problem would be reasonably done away with. In the course of blaming the "other," most people discussed them in broad terms: if only the liberals, conservatives, Democrats, Republicans, Libertarians would see how wrong they are, we could do something about this! Much was assumed about the other, and those assumptions fed the prejudices that then solidified the conviction that a certain group of people is to blame.

The convictions fed by our confirmation biases often help many people arrive at the conclusion that avoiding, undermining, or even fighting the other is a good way to begin fixing problems that we may encounter in living with the other. In essence, scapegoating blocks so much of our view that we are unable to see any solution other than one that involves finding a scapegoat. Our energies are then turned from searching for a solution to our problem to searching for reasons to support our choice of scapegoat. When we arrive at this point, we have confirmed and defined our prejudices of our own Samaria. From here on out, a swath of our new world is out of bounds as we look to figure out how to carve out a place in Samaria where we can keep it and Samaritans away. What's worse, because this Samaria has come as the result of negative prejudice, we also mistrust anything that could come from there.

What we are left with is that we are trying to carry out ministry with our hands tied behind our back intentionally. Once we have defined our Samaria and fed the mistrust that goes with that, we have lost a group of people as well as a deep well of ideas, support, and encouragement. Compounding that loss is that more often than not, we tend to place our Samarias precisely in the places where we probably most need to go.

Next to the church that I serve there is a closed funeral home. At the time that the story that follows took place, the owner was already fairly advanced in years and even more deeply set in his ways. This man started out serving his scapegoated community, the Italians. Our story begins back in the days when there was still some residual prejudice against that particular ethnicity. However, after some time the Italians too joined the local people, and most prejudices receded to occasional jokes said while spending time together. Business went well, and the man was able to purchase a fairly big building with the fantastic benefit of a parking lot. (Parking has been at a premium in the city since the beginning of the twentieth century.)

After a good many years of great business and becoming known in the community, the business began to experience changes in the surrounding neighborhood. At first it was just a trickle of African Americans, and though the owner didn't like it, his business didn't suffer too much; even those who had moved away because of the change still came back to him for their funeral needs. Then, in a matter of a decade, the trickle became a flood, and these flood-waters were then mixed with even less-wanted immigrants from Latin America. Throughout this time this man remained firm in deciding whom he would serve. He decided not to set foot in Samaria even though he found himself in the center of a Samaria of his own making.

Near the time of the closing of the funeral home I had a conversation with him that saddened me and confirmed in my mind that the funeral home was closing. One day there was a funeral at his business—an exception more than the norm by then. I noticed the activity, so I went outside. Because our church building is next to the funeral home, I mentioned to him that we could bring out our "no parking for funeral" signs so that the entire street side front of our church would be cleared for more people to park close to the funeral home. He responded by saying, "Yeah, can you tell your boy to do it?" I was confused because I didn't have a child then, and our sexton was a retired African American man. I said to him, "I think I can do it, and I can also ask our sexton, who is a retired man." He responded, "Yeah, your boy, tell him to bring them out." We discussed briefly how much I disagreed with his wording, but he just brushed it off and went on about his business. We were too busy to put our signs out to reserve parking for him. That was the last funeral I saw held in that funeral home.

That funeral home owner had to close his business because the town had been ruined by "those people" within twenty years. He chose to bleed money the last several years by keeping a business open without clientele. This man chose to see his business end rather than spend any significant amount of time with the Samaritans who had surrounded him. It doesn't seem that he ever considered how he contributed to the closing of his business.

We can choose to blame others, or we can look at our prejudices and deal with them constructively, as will be shown in the next chapter.

Notes
1. Douglas Adams, *The Prostitute in the Family Tree: Discovering Humor and Irony in the Bible* (Louisville: Westminster John Knox Press, 1997), 34.

2. David McRaney, *You Are Not So Smart: Why You Have Too Many Friends on Facebook, Why Your Memory Is Mostly Fiction, and 46 Other Ways You're Deluding Yourself* (New York: Gotham Books, 2011), 27.

3. René Girard, *I See Satan Fall Like Lightning*, trans. James G. Williams (Maryknoll, NY: Orbis Books, 2001).

CHAPTER 9

Letting Go

Straining forward to what lies ahead, I press on toward the goal for the prize of the heavenly call of God in Christ Jesus. Let those of us then who are mature be of the same mind; and if you think differently about anything, this too God will reveal to you. Only let us hold fast to what we have attained. (Philippians 3:13-16, NRSV)

When Nathanael was asked to join Jesus' community, he replied, "Can anything good come out of Nazareth?" (John 1:46, NRSV). For him, Jesus' hometown was a kind of Samaria. His prejudices about the place were so embedded within him that they spilled over onto everyone who came from there. I wonder how often church communities say that same thing about the places or people whom Jesus wants them to serve.

The Comfort of Prejudices and Assumptions

I have seen many people excitedly eat junk food after several days of eating strange food during mission trips. People who would never visit a fast-food joint at home joyfully enter the restaurant to order their burger and fries. Of course, the longer or farther we are from home, the more welcome a piece of home becomes—even if that piece of home is merely a McDonald's burger! Our prejudices have the comforting familiarity of the golden arches in a foreign country. Like McDonald's, our prejudices and assumptions offer the possibility of a bit of home when most needed.

As we settle into our Samaria, we will live through a period of feeling profoundly the strangeness of the new place. In the absence of home, we might be inclined to grasp at anything that can serve as a proxy for home. Because the type of journey that we are exploring involves being physically at home, our temptation to find rest and shelter will be sought in other ways. Such a situation then is primed for seeking the shelter of the known world that our assumptions can provide.

In Samaria, the ongoing work of the leader is to help the group members walk past their prejudices. Only self-reflection can help with the work of walking past assumptions and prejudices. Perhaps a journey to a familiar sight can illustrate self-reflection while we are in Samaria.

Admit the Extent of Our Prejudices

There will always be McDonald's moments when we move to a multicultural world. It would be silly to spend energy trying to avoid every McDonald's that we see, so how do we help people walk past the temptations? A first step is to admit that we will likely see every new place through the lens of our prejudices and assumptions. The purpose for admitting the extent of our prejudices is to begin changing the hurtful prejudices that we have created around being a Christian. These prejudices include thinking that we are better than those outside church. They also include believing that non-Christians are not as capable of good in the way Christians are. Additionally, by admitting some of our prejudices to our community, we can help everyone feel more comfortable about the fact that none of us is alone in having them.

Living with prejudices and erroneous assumptions is a normal state of life for all of us. So, as leaders, we can help those under our care to embrace the hope that we can deal with our prejudices rather than succumbing to the impossibility (given our imperfection) of eliminating them. We should not undermine or dismiss the struggle with coming to terms with the fact that we have been living with prejudices that we did not know existed, as they do help show us where we think we belong as well as help us know that we are no longer at home. However, Christ also leads us to know that home is not perfect. If even a Samaritan can be good, then we can give those whom we do not know a chance to prove our assumptions wrong.

Admit the Power of Our Prejudices

Another aspect of healthy self-reflection is to come to terms with the power that our assumptions and prejudices have over us. It is clear that Jesus chose a Samaritan because of the powerful prejudice that this group inspired in those listening to him. The parable was meant to show the quality of a good neighbor, but also to extend expectations beyond the border created by those listening to him. In other words, his Jewish audience needed to hear that the love that Jesus was talking about did not belong exclusively to them. The way Jesus chose to show that was by having good be done by a representative of a group of people whom the Jews thought of as incapable of the good that they saw as innate to themselves.

Please take a moment and think about who the Samaritans are for your congregation. Keep in mind that we are talking about the meaning that shocked the Jews listening to Jesus so much that the man who posed the question to Jesus couldn't even allow himself to say "Samaritan." Instead, the questioner responded, "The one who helped him." When we know how the Jews of that time saw Samaritans, we will be able to see the anger, irritation, or disappointment in that response. Ask yourself, "Who is my or our Samaritan here and now?"

Without self-reflection and honesty, our prejudices and assumptions can wield overwhelming power over us. Have you explored your prejudices and assumptions candidly enough to see that part of the reason you feel uncomfortable about the journey into Christian diversity is the power that these reactions toward the other have over you?

Many of the resources available to help churches find their way in a strange new world are based in a blame search. Generally, the process is to fill out questionnaires either about your ministries or the people in your neighborhood who are not being reached. Both options are ostensibly intended to help you discern what you lack as a church. Both items are important as part of the process, but without a journey of self-exploration we run the risk of doing a whole lot of work and ending up with little more than a clearer awareness that blame is with either "us" or "them."

By contrast, realizing why the familiarity of McDonald's affects us so much can take us a long way toward walking past it. To know that we are affected because we are feeling vulnerable, afraid of losing home, or worried that we will not be understood moves us to a more empowered position. Once we have discovered the root causes for our anxiety, we can begin to take charge of the problem and regain a sense of purpose and empowerment to change where we are.

When we have shifted from the power of prejudice to embrace a more self-empowered position, we begin to allow ourselves to see more options. We cease to be trapped by fear or anxiety about our circumstances and begin to explore our world more confidently. Dealing with root causes helps us to respond in more thought-out and effective ways. This small shift in attitude can be just enough for the leader to help your congregation walk past our McDonald's by pointing toward the better options just ahead. After all, if things do not work out, the home we have always known, including its McDonald's isn't going anywhere.

The Process of Discovery

By mentioning the good that is to come, we can help those we are leading begin to challenge the power that their assumptions and prejudices have over them. When I was a young child, I hated vegetables, any and all kinds of them. (Well, except for the radishes I planted in fourth grade at the village school I attended in Guatemala!) As I grew into adulthood, health and peer pressure forced me to begin eating vegetables again. What I discovered was a whole new world of flavors and foods that were good and healthy. It has now been long enough that I can spend time reflecting on the change. Through this process I discovered that the biggest problem I had with the foods that I could not eat had more to do with what they looked and felt like than their flavor. Of course, I don't love all vegetables now. Nor do I prefer a salad to an amazing burger. But now I can and do eat better. It took the journey of adulthood to make me realize there is food beyond McDonald's.

The process of discovery was not one that I particularly enjoyed, and it took a long time before I fully realized the benefits that come with my greater menu options. This type of change is not easy and should not be treated as if it were. Leaders may be tempted to gloss over difficulty in our attempts to enact change, but more often than not such strategy is counterproductive. It is much more productive to help the church rediscover that difficulties are part of worthwhile experiences.

Expecting difficulties to be part of the process is an uphill battle in our current world. Our society tells us that difficulties are to be avoided. It is our right not to suffer under difficulties, so we should not put up with them. What ends up happening is that many of us tend to go with the path of least resistance or try to walk around the difficulties rather than work through them. However, an appealing shortcut is almost always too good to be true.

Several years ago I was part of a group that was exploring church growth methods around our country. We visited a church that had seen explosive growth in the previous five years. After a day or so of hearing about increase in numbers and the need to purchase a bigger space, we finally got to sit down and chat with the pastor who had led the transition. He began by saying (unknowingly echoing the pastor who tried G12), "When we chose to go this way, I was left with three people in church." He had chosen to leave the past behind and get rid of anything that would get in the way.

Then we discovered that the growth had not come from the church's efforts alone. They had joined the popular Latin American church movement that had become a well-oiled machine designed for profits for the top. In essence, the program works with small groups and offers various perks for the small-group leaders that increase as the leader creates more small groups. All of that came with a fairly sizable initial investment from the organization. Any church that joins gets financial and people support in the beginning for a certain period of time. After that initial period the church then has to begin "offering" back the investment that it was given and then keep giving for the sake of the "Kingdom." One other interesting aspect of this church was that it had a fairly large turnover ratio. In any case, if the church does not grow enough to begin repaying, the organization withdraws the help and the church is left with nothing.

On the surface, this type of growth seems extremely appealing. Can you imagine your struggling church going from forty people to four hundred in three years? But far from fostering change from transformation, it simply replaces one church with another. In many ways it is like skipping McDonald's to go on to Burger King.

The Difficulty of Letting Go

The love that we have for our past can and often does sustain us in times of crisis. Faithful people throughout our country live with a church past that is so important that it often takes precedence over the present and the future. Often our mistake is that we don't acknowledge to them the importance of the past with which they are living. Expressions such as "That's not how we do it," "We've never done it that way before," and "That's not how things are done" speak to something deeper than being trapped by tradition. Many times the foundation on which those assertions rest is the deeply felt love for the church that they now feel slipping away. Therefore, any time we ask people to let go of something, we need to do so gently and with deep awareness of the pain that the process will cause. We cannot rip the love of their faith lives away from them suddenly if we want to help the church continue.

When Moses guided the Israelites into their own journey of freedom, difficulties came very quickly. When they faced the expanse of the desert and uncertainty about their journey, many Israelites were willing to go back to being slaves. They even spoke longingly of that time: "If only we had died by the hand of the LORD in Egypt, when we sat by the fleshpots and ate our fill of bread; for you have brought us out into this wilderness to kill this whole assembly with hunger" (Exodus 16:3, NRSV). If letting go is so bad, why should we?

What Does It Mean to Let Go?

As we all know, "to let go" can easily become soaked with the group's anxieties during times of transition. A leader must be intentional about the process of education regarding the meaning of that expression, as well as the emotional entanglements embedded in the action. So, we should begin with the educational aspect of what it means to let go. After we have learned about healthy ways to let go, we can create a process that works for the church or the group.

The first step in our education is highlighting that without real information about something, imagination and gossip take over, and soon the information vacuum is filled with hearsay and projected anxiety. It behooves the leader to work hard to define letting go with the appropriate information that we have received from Scripture. As we see with the Israelites during the exodus, when difficulty came, their first instinct was to look back longingly to the life from which they were saved because of their crying out to God. Their reaction highlights the importance of faith in the process of letting go. Pointing back to the faith on which our entire trip depends will be helpful throughout. We have decided to go because of God's call. We trust that, as with the exodus, God goes before us and will care for us through to the promised land.

After time and work on rekindling our faith, during this difficult section of the journey we can also discuss what it means to let go in the context of our journey. First, our journey is not one to recapture the idealized past. Second, we need to remind those we are leading that letting go does not mean that the past is always bad or the enemy.

To Let Go Is Not to Forget

It seems like many of the full-on contemporary churches are discovering that church is much more than just an elaborate worship experience with professional video, graphics, and music band. There have always been small group aspects to these churches, but those experiences often served to reinforce what happened on Sunday mornings. Or, they were closer to self-help therapy groups than fellowship spaces where relationships with God and each other were deepened. This rediscovery is moving the need for deep relational ties up in the priorities list for these churches and thus bringing them back to looking to learn from the deep well of church tradition regarding close, deep fellowship.

As with every movement, it is difficult to identify the whole by a name, but many of them call themselves "church 2.0."[1] So church 2.0 is like church but better. Church 2.0 is a place where people know the value of deep relationships and the importance of church being a deeply involved member of the community that makes a difference locally. We have discovered that it is not just God and myself.

These "new" discoveries can happen only because at some point we thought that in order to let go of the bad in church, we had to forget it all and start afresh. Many places throw the baby out with the bathwater—to use an older expression—when they see letting go of the past as doing away with it. In our teaching of what it means to let go as a follower of Christ, we have to clarify the distinction between letting go as getting rid of something and letting go as placing the past in its appropriate place of respect and usefulness.

To let go, therefore, is not to do away with the past as though it were not important. We are not asking the church to forget and throw away its past. We are asking the church to allow the past to remain where it belongs and stop trying to bring it forward to a place where it is not meant to be and where it cannot survive. Our journey into the new is not a rejection of the past, but rather is an addition to it that will allow us to engage with the new world without losing who we are.

To let go is to move toward freedom by opening space for ourselves to see the world with new eyes, to feel free to look at our new world without the need to have it be as good as our often idealized past. We are free to engage with our world while carrying fewer prejudices. Imagine seeing the world around as it is rather than mainly for what it isn't anymore. If you have trouble picturing the wonder of such an event, watch a new movie with a child. Observe how the child is free to enjoy the entirely new experience without hang-ups such as "the original was better" or "this is just a bad version of that other movie I saw when I was younger."

Letting go in the way I have been discussing here also opens up much-needed room for us to journey toward forgiveness of ourselves as well as those around us. As we noted, the need to find blame seems to be part of the human experience. Therefore, it is not a stretch to imagine that most churches that are in deep crisis have a list of scapegoats that they see at fault for what has happened. Just as likely, few in those places are willing to discuss those to blame openly. So, we hang on to our past as well as the self-blame or blaming that comes with having witnessed nearly constant decline that is as close as ever to closing the church. When we let go in an appropriate way, we begin to see possibilities that could indeed include forgiveness. It is remarkable how much energy is spent on maintaining grievances or hurt year after year. Forgiveness as part of letting go gives us a chance to be free from such a heavy load.

How to Let Go

Be aware that this process will be difficult. You will need to give it as much time as necessary. So, when we think about how to let go, as leaders we must remember to be aware of the community as well as the individual. As with most important things in life, one-size-fits-all is not enough for most of us.

Having said that, I can offer a path that is both broad enough to provide flexibility to the local leader and well-marked enough to serve as a roadmap for individuals and communities.

Recovery

I have named this part of the process "recovery" because if up to this point we have walked in this journey as honestly as possible, then we should be at a place where we need to recover. We have been through a journey of guided self-reflection that has led us toward focusing on our faults by way of exposing emotions, attitudes, and prejudices that we have covered with layers of justification. The journey has been difficult, long, and painful. Worse yet, all we have to show for it is that we find ourselves in a foreign land! We are tired, lost, and frustrated but still not at our new home.

We are indeed in need of recovery. Letting go is a tough thing to do. We cannot start again as though we have not been hurt, disappointed, or saddened. Plan for a recovery period in which comfort, love, assurance, and support are abundantly present. With that thought in mind, we can explore a three-step plan: clarify, explore, and mourn.

Clarify. Let us begin our process of recovery by making sure that we are all as close to being on the same page as possible. Clarifying where we are makes it easier to begin recovery by showing us what we need. The path of clarification gives us a chance to make sure that we have been letting go in a healthy way. This is our chance to review what it means to give up those things that are holding us back without giving up who we are. We need to share with one another what it is that we feel must be let go and agree on how to care for those things that are now a part of our memory, secure as part of our rich history where it belongs.

While walking the path of clarification, we can remind our people that giving up those things that are holding us back does not mean giving up on our past or trying to forget who we were. Letting go of unnecessary burdens is not the same as discarding our past and starting with a clean slate. As we saw in the story about square dancing, we need to leave square dancing in the past as a great memory, but it does not mean that the purpose for the square dancing also needs to be left behind (see chapter 4). In other words, it is healthy to let go of the way we did things for the sake of the purpose for which those things were done.

Explore. After walking through clarification for a bit, we will come to a small clearing where we can sit and explore the resulting feelings. Here leaders can help the community take the time to explore the feelings resulting from letting go. We can ask questions such these: What do you think is affecting you most about letting go? Is it that you loved the things that were done? Could it be that keeping those things alive also keeps alive the memory of the people who were there? (For example, does the idea of moving pews feel like giving up on the memory of the spouse with whom you sat in the same place for forty years?)

The process of exploring our feelings in community must be led intentionally by someone. The leader must listen intently and guide the conversation gently by using probing and open-ended questions. Dig deeper toward exploring that which affects us the most. Why do you feel that you are so affected by the change in the order of service? Press through the remaining justifications toward the root cause.

During this exploration, remember that this process needs to be cushioned by healthy amounts of comfort and loving assurances. I should make clear here that "comfort" does not mean absence of pain. Rather, comfort is necessary in the *presence* of pain, because it creates a space in which vulnerable people can feel safe enough to share their difficulties. Please, avoid superficial assurances such as saying that all will be okay without explaining how. Instead, we want to assure our people that this process is the healthy way forward in our journey home.

Mourn. An intentional and honest exploration of our feelings can bring us closer to the root causes for our feelings of loss, frustration, and anxiety. In turn, recognition of those root causes can lead us to a place where we can mourn our losses in a way that helps us say good-bye. Letting go requires a time for lament because we are leaving behind things that have sustained us for decades. People need a mourning process when they feel that all that is dear to them has been slowly taken away.

As leaders, we have to find creative ways to mark the passing of something that has been dearly held for a long time. I could provide examples of what to do here, but you, as the local leader, are best suited to develop these. Mourning is a private thing that should be done first with those closest to us. It is in the intimacy of meaningful community that we can find the best ways to say goodbye. So, lead your people from the valley of exploration into mourning in a way that lets all grieve without the pressing need to move on for the moment.

Reengaging

There is a time for everything (Ecclesiastes 3:1-8). There is a time to grieve and a time to move into a new place and begin making it home. Grieving a loss is sorely needed in our culture because most of us are too busy trying to get on with life. But few things are as good for our emotional health as moving toward reengaging life after grieving appropriately. Of course, the sense of loss does not go away, nor is the emptiness filled in as though it was never there. Yet, by grieving in a healthy way we can leave the crippling sense of guilt behind. By grieving well we are freer to look forward without fears of being uncaring or disrespectful to our past and loved ones who are gone. This type of freedom comes not from forgetting or discarding but from holding the past in its proper place.

We have had to take a long and painful journey because our new place is very much the old one but different in important ways. The physical sameness between our old and new home could keep us from moving on without self-reflection and mourning. Because our emotions do not change overnight, reengagement needs to happen after a period of recovery. That period of recovery ends with our mourning season.

When our past has been brought into an appropriate and healthy perspective, we can begin to reengage with the world around us. We will still miss the old home at times, but our exploration of the new home can now be from an expectant and hopeful place. We know that we can adjust and move on, so we can look around our world in hopeful expectation. These new lenses can help us to see more of the good of what is around us, as well as be at peace with knowing that we can live with the new. Go, explore this new world as a child arriving at a new playground. You will fall and maybe even get hurt, but remember: God's watchful eye is always with you.

Notes
1. See Randy Frazee, *The Connecting Church 2.0: Beyond Small Groups to Authentic Community* (Grand Rapids: Zondervan, 2013).

CHAPTER 10

Following Jesus

Go therefore and make disciples of all nations, baptizing them in the name of the Father and of the Son
and of the Holy Spirit. (Matthew 28:19, NRSV)

Jesus came for the whole world. The Gospels are filled with
accounts of Jesus' love for all of God's children. Indeed, the entire
New Testament attests to Jesus' call to us all to follow in his foot-
steps. Though many passages exemplify for us Jesus' call to love
the world, few do so in the way that Matthew 28:18-20 recounts
Jesus' clarion call to his disciples. The best-known sentence from
that encounter is known as the Great Commission: "Go therefore
and make disciples of all nations."

As leaders in the church, we know how powerful that call was
and is. It is no exaggeration to say that the call from Jesus changed
the world in profound ways. To enumerate how the world has
been changed by the Great Commission is beyond the scope of this
or any book. However, what is relevant to this book is how the
power of that call drove a few small-town Jews to set about reaching the world.

What gave such power to those words said so long ago was
Jesus' presence. By the time we arrive at the mountaintop where
these words were said, Jesus and his disciples had lived through a
lifetime of extraordinary events in the span of around three years.

During that time Jesus was a permanent and assuring presence through the difficulties, great times, and boring hours of traveling. The one time he left his disciples, he did so after he had explained to them why he had to leave. But even then, he left them with a promise to return three days later. By the time we find the disciples meeting Jesus at this mountaintop moment, he has fulfilled his promise to return. Jesus had a long and established record of fulfilling his promises to his community of disciples. The presence of Jesus with them during ministry and at this particular encounter gave so much power to his words that we are reaping the benefits to this day.

The relationship born through the presence that Jesus had with his disciples was the foundation on which the world was changed. The trust and faith born during their time with Jesus fed the fire with which they set about carrying out his call to them. Correspondingly, the impetus that moves us into a journey toward Christian multiculturalism and the strength that sustains us through the change will be as strong as the relationship that leads us to call ourselves Christians. It is from the depth of our Christian identity, born from profound relationship, that the call from Jesus draws its strength to effect changes within us, changes that empower the few to transform the world around them.

The power of the call has not diminished, because the One on whom that power rests is with us still: "And remember, I am with you always, to the end of the age" (Matthew 28:20, NRSV). The Jesus who loved more deeply and indiscriminately than anyone else has also kept all his promises. He still stands by that call and loves and supports all who answer. That same power can still birth life even in forgotten churches left behind by the world.

The journey that we are undertaking depends heavily on reencountering that call as closely as we can to the way the disciples heard it on that day. How did the disciples hear Jesus' call?

As a starting point, the disciples could be clear that Jesus came to save the whole world. The Gospels testify to that universal mission and unambiguously call us to imitate the expansiveness of God's love: "For God so loved the world" (John 3:16, NRSV). As if those words were not enough, Jesus elsewhere illustrated the depth and breadth of that call by asking us to love others as ourselves; in other words, to love them as equals. Jesus' actions consistently bear witness to God's stated purpose of coming for the sake of all.

When the disciples heard the words of the Great Commission, they did so as members of an oppressed people, living in the margins of the world. Worse still, Jesus himself had been punished in a way reserved for the worst political traitors. These people had good reason to fear for their lives, yet they heard that instead of hiding or fighting they were to love all, including those who had placed them in this predicament. They were to love those whom they did not like. Jesus' call was even asking them to love those who were oppressing them, because the Romans were part "of all nations."

The call, like Jesus' ministry, turned assumptions upside down. Rather than finding victory in revenge, the disciples were to find victory in loving the adversary so profoundly that their love changes the relationship. The oppressed people were called to love as their response to oppression.

The power of the call lived in the presence of Jesus. His words to the disciples changed the world because of his presence and their relationship with one another. Jesus' presence in community with them was the power that filled his words with all that the disciples needed to change the world. The community that was born with Jesus' call and time with the disciples was where the disciples were encouraged, sustained, and empowered to carry out the ministry entrusted to them. The power of Jesus' call sat on the strength of their relationship with God and surrounded them through their relationship with the community. Because the power of the call relies in the depth of our relationship with Jesus, how are we, so far away from that day, to find a way to recapture the power of that experience?

Checking Our Relationship with Jesus

Perhaps we can begin by checking in on our relationship with Jesus. This self-check must be profound and honest. Let us look at our church and ourselves and aim to see past our justifications for our distance from God. For example, many of us have cherished the wonder of the love of God for humankind, but too often our expression of that love has become increasingly limited and isolated to our own little world. In our smaller world, church has become either a refuge from the world or the place where we are refreshed by wonderful worship brought to us by well-crafted services aided by the best that we can afford in talent and technology. The former is a small, insular place that is a shelter from the world; the latter is a church that teaches self-love where we leave our Sunday services or midweek gatherings feeling better about ourselves. Either of those options tends to help us craft an image of Jesus tailor-made for ourselves but often far from the Christ we ought to follow.

Where is your relationship with Jesus? How close is your church to Jesus? Checking in on our relationship with Jesus lets us know where we are. This self-check is not a search for blame. The self-check is a means to help us begin the process of rekindling the fire of presence that gives power to the Great Commission.

Many times we may find ourselves discovering that we have drifted away from God. That distance from God is often an unsuspected culprit in difficulties at church. Part of the problem is that many of us in church have had a profound and meaningful relationship with Jesus, but we have not seen him in a while. Worries about a changed world, old buildings, a dwindling congregation, or explosive growth all conspire to shift our focus from Christ. The further away our focus moves, the less we see of Christ and the more we see our image of Christ.

Of course, as humans, we are imperfect, and that imperfection makes relationships with even those around us in the flesh difficult to keep up. Yet, many of us lead a life with Jesus where we spend time with God for only one or maybe a couple of hours per week. Given that relationships take time and presence, it is not difficult to see how spending one or two hours per week with Jesus is not enough to lead to a deeper relationship with God. The problem with drifting away is that this distance may leave us with a Jesus who looks more like the one we want to remember than the one calling to us from Matthew's Gospel.

Adding to our difficulty in coming closer to Jesus is the fact that the church, in its attempt to listen to the people, seems to be moving toward a market-driven approach to becoming relevant. This consumerist view of church has been a difficult challenge at our congregation. We often hear about how impressed and grateful people are concerning the work we are doing at our church in Norristown. At the same time, we hear about good people with leadership qualities being warned about coming to our congregation because we may put them to work right away. Better to go to a bigger church that has a staff to do the work. After all, at a bigger church one can do only the things that are convenient and do not interrupt one's schedule. When we treat God's children like clients, they will treat us like they hired us.

To be at a place where we only worship or give our leftover time places us even further away from the depth of emotion and connection that are intrinsic to the power of the call from Jesus. The disciples heard that call while facing the danger of physical and spiritual death; they had brought such danger upon themselves by virtue of their unconditional following of Jesus. They had walked with him while wounded, and shared the risks as well as the joys of his ministry. Their relationship with Jesus was deep enough for them to be asked to change the world.

By limiting our relationship with Jesus to convenience, we drift away into the shallows where there are no waves but also no growth. The distance, which often happens imperceptibly, can draw us away from Jesus and toward the pressures of everyday life. Therefore, a constant check on our relationship with Jesus must be part of our life as Christians. Conveniently, checking in allows us to find out where we are as well as to begin the process of rekindling the relationship on our way to deepening it.

One way by which we can begin deepening our relationship with Jesus is by allowing our Christian identity to permeate our lives.

My appearance is that of a Latino person. I also spent a good deal of my formative years in Central America. As a result, I carry with me visual and auditory cues that speak to my origin. So, invariably when I meet people, we always get to "Where are you from?" Given my background, it is difficult to give a clear answer, so I generally default to the area where I am living. Currently my response is "I'm from Pennsylvania." It's obvious that sometimes people are surprised by that response. Often the next question is "Well, but *where* are you from?"

You see, my life has influenced so deeply who I am that wherever I am my accent betrays me. However much I try to fit in, there is always something in me that betrays the otherness within. I do not have a heavy accent; in fact, those who know me well are often surprised by the suggestion that I have an accent at all. Yet, I cannot escape my cultural identity, and in time I have come to embrace it as part of who I am.

In a similar sense, I wonder how much of our Christian identity betrays us to those around. Notice the use of the word "betray." I choose to use that word because what I mean is something beyond our intentional attempts at letting people know that we are Christian. Does your walk with Jesus show even when you are not trying to have it show? What about in the supermarket, on the bus or train, on the job, behind the wheel of a car? Or when what you ordered at the restaurant is not what the server brings you? Or when a sign says "open" but the worker says that the store is closed?

Does your Christian identity show in regular life? In other words, is your Christianity second nature? There is good theology in many of our old hymns and songs. One truth that convicts me often is this: "And they'll know we are Christians by our love." Our Christian identity surfaces not by the big Bible that we carry or even by the way we tell people that Jesus loves them. Is carrying a Bible or evangelizing others wrong? Of course not! But, can we say that our life as a Christian has so influenced who we are that wherever we are our "accent" betrays us?

How Do We Come Closer to Jesus?

Because the power of Jesus' call is drawn from presence and close relationship, we know that we need to walk along the path that leads to hearing the call from Jesus. The language of journey takes on particular relevance as we come to explore the context of how the Great Commission was given to the disciples. It comes to them at the culmination of a journey. The call came near the completion of Jesus' ministry on earth. The disciples arrived after a worrisome stage of their journey with him, beginning with Jesus' arrest, trial, and crucifixion. They had to climb a mountain to arrive at the meeting place. To top it all off, the moment came after they had spent years in a journey of intense fellowship and discipleship with Jesus. They had walked a path with and toward Jesus for years before they came to the moment of hearing the call. So too must we journey toward Jesus in humble discipleship.

Our name speaks to the journey in response to Jesus' call. The English word "Christian" comes from the Greek *Christianos* (see

Acts 11:26; 26:28; 1 Peter 4:16), which means "follower of Christ." There is action in our name! We are born in faith but become who we are as the result of following Jesus. Our history as a church speaks to that active following. Throughout most of its history the understanding of that word has been deeply tied to profound change resulting from faith. That faith leads to following Christ in word and deed. As the well-known song so clearly puts it, "And they'll know we are Christians by our love."

Still, we may ask: How can we deepen our relationship with Christ? The first step is to come to Scripture and live into that through the experience of community. Meditating on Scripture in community on Sunday mornings, in Bible studies, Sunday school class, and other experiences can help us begin the journey.

There is another wonderful road we can take alongside Scripture. In Spanish there is an expression that roughly means, "In remembering we live again" (*Recordar es volver a vivir*). By remembering the Gospel stories and sharing our experiences, we can help ourselves feel the real presence of God in our midst more deeply. Recounting the beauty and power of a call birthed in love and freely shared with us is inspiring and even exciting. Many of us are refreshed and encouraged by that love weekly when we gather together to worship by singing, reading, and learning. The more real Christ is in our lives, the deeper our relationship with God will grow.

More often than we may like, the joy and excitement that we experience on Sunday mornings may go only as far as the middle of the week. Then, as the time of worshiping in community recedes, the weights of the reality of our fallen world can overshadow the remembrance. The load of setbacks, loss of people, the challenges of aging or ill health, and other difficulties conspire to put a strain on our ability and even our desire to do the work of deepening our relationship with God. Such weight alone can often feel like too much to bear.

When we add to those common burdens the challenge of a journey to Samaria—having to move toward something that we are not sure we like—the burden can become too taxing. But let us not be discouraged, because to revisit the call from the Scriptures can encourage and inspire us to start walking our faith again.

As we have noted, the church has been sitting in increasing discomfort and isolation for too long. It is time for us to move, to be inspired, to pick up our cross and follow Jesus' leading, a leading that often takes us to the very Samaria we do not want to visit. There have always been exceptions, but on the whole, being a Christian has been faith leading to action as a goal if not always a lived reality. Growing closer to Jesus does shake us into actions of love for all.

In this walk we also do well to remember that there is an inherent struggle between being a Christian as Scriptures call us to be and the pressures of a culture that prizes self-reliance and independence. In our culture, success is often defined by individual achievements. For an example of this we need look no further than how the biggest churches in our country often are identified most closely with the name of their celebrity pastor. One of the dangers of seeing success in this way is that it depends on the abilities, charisma, or star power of individuals. Many of us have been so permeated by this limited definition of success that we do not even realize that we are looking to make the church in our image rather than seeking to reflect who God is to the world. I once chatted with a church planter who said to me, "I want to be the Latino Rick Warren." The struggle to balance being a humble follower with the societal pressures to be self-sufficient continues to affect us negatively at church.

In some significant ways the young and successful Christians of today are doing the same thing that our grandparents and parents did: transforming people into what *we* think they should be. Falling into the desire to fashion a church after our own image is not limited to old or new, experienced or new Christians. Recall my interviews with potential new ministers of music, all of whom were dismissive of the idea of using the organ in our early worship service (see the introduction). None of us is free of the temptation of wanting to have a church after our own image. Therefore, we must accept that the struggle between what we learn about self-reliance from the world in which we live and what it means to follow Christ wholeheartedly will be a constant companion in our journey.

Given this struggle, we need to be more creative about the ways we deepen our relationship with God as we replenish spiritually during our journey. To that end, the next chapter will explore more deeply the guidance that we receive from Scripture, particularly the Gospels. It is my hope that by spending time with their account of Jesus' ministry, we can gather a clearer picture of his leading for us as individuals and community. Spending more time in Scripture will help us see who it is that we should reach out to, as well as how and why, as we follow Jesus' call to love our neighbor as ourselves.

CHAPTER 11

Loving Others

> I give you a new commandment, that you love one
> another. Just as I have loved you, you also should love
> one another. By this everyone will now that you are
> my disciples, if you have love for one another. (John
> 13:34-35, NRSV)

In this particular part of our journey we will find ourselves
briefly living with several key archetypes that we find in the
Gospel stories as stand-ins for the *other*. My hope is that in
spending time with them we can find encouragement and guidance for our journey. The struggles that we find in those stories
can illustrate for us the difficulty in welcoming the other into our
intimate worlds. Revisiting the experiences of these archetypes
in the Gospels can inspire the hope that we too can participate
in Jesus' active love of all regardless of who they are or who we
think they should be.

Who Is the Other?

Karl Barth, in *The Humanity of God*, explores the breadth of
God's call to love all as equal. This is a great way to introduce the
core of the discussion in this chapter, the Gospel imperatives
regarding community. What did Jesus say about the other?

Nameless (Mark 1:34)

From the beginning, Jesus' ministry challenged everyone around him. The breadth of his ministry reached out even to the nameless. In first-century Palestine, it was important to know someone's name in order to be able to place people in their appropriate slot in society. Otherwise, one could be associating with someone who could hurt one's reputation. Yet, Jesus never hesitated to help those without name. Many stories depict Jesus stopping and placing in the center of his story some nameless person. The man with an unclean spirit interrupts Jesus' ministry at the synagogue (Mark 1:21-28). A blind man was brought to Jesus at Bethsaida (Mark 8:22-26). In Mark 5:21-43 we find the story of a woman and a girl who are not mentioned by name, even though they are at the center of the events described there. How many more nameless people can you find in the Gospels?

Years ago I was at a touristy resort town. While walking around, my friends and I came upon a group of attractive young girls handing out flyers as they chatted with people. As we came closer, one of them approached me and handed me a flyer as she started talking. I noticed right away that the flyer had a picture of a dark-skinned child. I did not read the flyer because she was giving me the sales pitch for helping children who live in hunger. As she talked, I noticed how passionate she was about her cause. So, after her speech and when I was just about ready to give all the cash I had, I asked her where these children were. She responded, "They are all around us, man!" When I pressed for more information, it became clear that she had not helped any of these hungry children directly. Our world helps us to be able to feel better about ourselves by helping the nameless without having to spend time with them. Jesus came close to the nameless, and so should we.

Lepers (Matthew 8:1-3; Luke 17:11-19)

The call to love our neighbor means that the list of the unworthy, unclean, and undeserving is eliminated. In the process of modeling love for everyone, Jesus spent time with people thought to have been cursed by either their own sin or that of their parents. Lepers lived out their lives in eternal punishment for something that they had nothing to do with yet was assumed to be a punishment from God for a sin committed. Not only did they die a horrible, slow death, but also the entire time they were on their way to that death they had to live with the corpse of their relationships. They were unclean, so they had to keep away from everyone. If someone was approaching a leper from the opposite direction, the leper had to warn that person to stay away. In the passage from Luke we see how, while keeping their distance, the lepers called out to Jesus pleading for mercy from him. Jesus again responds as though he meant what he said, and he cleansed them. God's forgiveness is such that it can pardon and cure even a leper.

I wonder who are the lepers in your church community—those people who are condemned by the good people as bad and pushed to the fringes. What does your community treat as though it were as contagious as leprosy and as incurable? Our list so far would have already made the majority of people hearing Jesus' message uncomfortable. Could it get any worse?

Tax Collectors (Mark 2:13-17)

Jesus did not simply greet tax collectors and serve them on occasion. Wayne Jackson notes, "He let them 'draw near' to him (Luke 15:1), went into their homes (Luke 19:5), sat with them (Matthew 9:10), ate with them (Matthew 9:11), and was a 'friend' to these despicable people (Matthew 11:19; Luke 7:34)."[1]

There was no love lost between Jesus' disciples and tax collectors. These people were robbing from good people for the sake of an occupying empire as well as their own greed. Yet, Jesus sought to spend time with them. He even invited one tax collector, Matthew, to be a disciple (Matthew 9:9-13). He did not begin his encounters by telling tax collectors how bad they were. When he saw Zacchaeus, his first words to him were to express clearly his desire to come to Zacchaeus's house. Mark 2 also shows Jesus spending time with these despicable people. Nowhere in these encounters do we find Jesus beginning his relationship with them in judgment.

Many of our churches seem to default to telling people first how wrong they are and second how good we at the church are. When we go to a restaurant and leave a tract instead of a tip, we are not seen as loving people. When our treatment of others clearly lets them know that we think ourselves better than them, we are not loving. When we place conditions of repentance on others in order to relate to them, we are not following Jesus.

The town of Norristown, Pennsylvania, has been living with a first wave of immigration from Latin America for the last ten to fifteen years. It had been more than one hundred years since this town had experienced the difficulties of living through a wave of immigration. Nonetheless, there are many churches lovingly trying to do what they can to help the new, underserved people. A big need in this area is English classes. However, many of the churches that help also place preconditions for these free classes. Mainly, people have to sit through a Bible study either before or after the class in order to attend. Some of the people eventually join the church, but I believe that they would have joined anyway. What I wonder about is the other people who now know that nothing is free at that church. To many of these people, churches may come to be seen as tax collectors: their purpose for relating with you is to get something from you.

Samaritans (John 4:1-27)

The nameless, lepers, and even tax collectors were not beyond Jesus' call to love all. Still, Jesus was not done pushing the boundaries of who is acceptable and welcomed as a child of God. Jesus went straight past a well-known and respected line and kept going all the way out to the Samaritans. He showed by his actions that he came for everyone, even the hated Samaritans.

The enmity between Jews and Samarians went on for hundreds of years. Each side believed in God deeply and hated the other side almost equally. They both had desecrated each other's sacred spaces, and for Jews, just being near a Samaritan could render one impure. Samaria was an area to be avoided even if it made a journey twice as long. It is difficult to exaggerate the hatred between these groups. The misreading of Jesus' intent in the parable of the good Samaritan has dulled the power of the parable so much that now we think that the rescuer's Samaritan identity is not very relevant to the lesson of the parable. Such understanding makes us miss the point of the parable. Jesus wanted to extend the existence of "good" so far beyond comfort that he used as an example a Samaritan, who for Jews embodied that which was to be despised. At the same time, the uncaring ones in the parable, a priest and a Levite, were those most admired by the listeners. With this parable Jesus made clear that our established, cherished, and respected walls of separation stand in the way of what he was trying to achieve. God's goodness and love can be seen even in, especially in, Samaritans.

I wonder whose presence would make you want to leave your church. The problem with the parable of the good Samaritan is that it is clear that Jesus wants us to love and see the good in those whom we do not respect or may even hate. The point of the story is not that good was done but that good came from a place where we feel it should not. So, as you are preparing for your journey toward multiculturalism, are you including Samaritans in your planning? When the church growth books and consultants tell you that the demographics of your area say that for the greatest chance of success you should be a family church, a young professionals church, or other, will you reply, "But what about the Samaritans?" Unclean women, prostitutes, tax collectors, lepers, a Roman soldier, even Samaritans were welcomed by Jesus. There is no room for misunderstanding. Throughout his ministry Jesus was always proving that he meant what he said by doing it. For God so loved the world, indeed!

Scripture shows us how those around Jesus were made extremely uncomfortable by his reaching out to all. It is obvious that this stretching was difficult for even his closest disciples. The journey toward embracing all is not easy and is often painful. I say this not to discourage but to encourage us all to expect discomfort and pain. I think that we all have had enough of a shallow perception of church growth as something that should be fun and full of laughter, as it is often portrayed in church growth posters. The disciples were constantly bothered by Jesus' choices of people to visit. Could you imagine what it took for a faithful Jew like Peter not only to enter the house of a tax collector but also to break bread with him?

We All Bring Baggage

We all bring baggage on our climb to the mountaintop to which Jesus has called us to meet him. In every instance, we find Jesus willingly engaging with people who have been cast out of society or have been set up as antagonists to good society. This change cannot be easy for anyone around Jesus: disciples, witnesses, those following along. Everyone watching these interactions was carrying the baggage of their own culture and the prejudices against the people to whom Jesus was speaking. Therefore, each of the people mentioned in these Scriptures had to carry double weight. All of them had to carry the pain from their own illness or reason for being made an outcast, as well as pain and baggage projected on them by the Jewish community of that time. Therefore, when the call from Jesus to go to all people comes at the mountaintop, it ought to feel as daunting to us as it must have felt to the disciples on that day so long ago (Matthew 28:16-20). The closer we are to

Jesus, the more difficult it is likely to feel, because the memory of who Jesus reached out to should be fresh in our minds. So, all the people onto whom we project our baggage are placed squarely in our way and perhaps even made our destination. Thankfully, Jesus has encouraged us to bring Him our baggage instead of only sharing it with each other (Matthew 11:28).

Being close to Jesus, immediately we know that the call means going into Samaria. Jesus wants us not only to talk to but also ask to eat with tax collectors. When Jesus gives the call, it includes the possibility of standing between an accusing crowd and the sinner accused by them (John 7:53–8:11). Jesus' call demands that we stop for the unclean and help, even if it is a leper or, worse, someone not even worthy of having a name. This call is the call to love all, especially those whom we want to make exceptions because their presence in our home offends us.

The call would be too rough, too demanding, too raw for us sinners without Jesus' promise in Matthew 28:20: "I am with you always." The importance of a close, deep relationship with Jesus is a must if we are to follow his call in deed as well as word. It is the strength of that relationship that gives power to the promise. The assurance of God's presence and the profound knowledge of what that means may well be exactly what we need to be moved past our fears into loving action. "But God proves his love for us in that while we still were sinners Christ died for us" (Romans 5:8).

Dealing with Hurt and Pain

Admittedly, the pain of moving beyond our comfort zone still remains. Therefore, as we bring this gospel imperative to love all to our communities, there are many things that must be addressed. Chief among them is the ability to deal with hurt and pain in a healthy way. It is not wise to try to find a way around having to live into, with, through, or past hurt, pain, and fear. We must ask the difficult questions, such as "What prevents us from relating to a particular group in our community?" As we lead others through this section of our journey, we must remember that the pain that many people feel is real, whether the hurt was real or only perceived.

If "salvation lies in the memory of wrongs suffered," as Miroslav Volf says, "it must lie more in what we do with those memories than in the memories themselves."[2] The power of our past is such that it influences the choices of many people in the present. Our reaction to the new is therefore rarely free from the influence of our past. Churches do not escape this fate and, like individuals, often live in ignorance of how much the memory of wrongs suffered influences choices made. In the process of discussing how to deal with the past, Volf provides four possible ways of engaging with our past. First, memory can be a means to healing. Second, acknowledging memory can be a means of salvation. Third, memory can birth solidarity. Fourth, memory can be a means of protection. Let us explore these four ways through which Volf seeks to help us remember well.

Memory can be a means to healing. Many people are oppressed by things in their past that they refuse to acknowledge or deal with. I know that Sigmund Freud has fallen out of favor in many ways, and rightly so, but I think that he was correct when he wrote, "An unexpressed traumatic experience is like an invasive pathogen which long after its entry must continue to be regarded as an agent that is still at work."[3] Many times the walk with people toward a more Kingdom-like outlook on the world includes that difficult trip back to painful memories.

Acknowledgment is also another way through which memory can be another means of salvation. "If no one remembers a misdeed or names it publicly, it remains invisible."[4] The victims get lost, and perpetrators continue to harm others and themselves. Victims need to be heard: "Since remembering wrongs is an act that acknowledges them, it is therefore an act of justice."[5]

Another way remembering can serve as a means of salvation is by generating solidarity with the victims. Remembering suffering can awaken us from our slumber of indifference and urge us to fight against the suffering and oppression around us. We forget our history at our own peril. Those who do not revisit their history are doomed to repeat it. For example, the civil rights movement had many powerful and eloquent advocates. Few were as powerful as the peaceful demonstrators whose clothes and skin were torn by police dogs. Solidarity was given a voice when those events were replayed on television screens for the whole nation to see.

The last way remembering can be a means of salvation is that it can bring protection. Eli Wiesel, in his Nobel Prize lecture, said, "Memory of evil will serve as a shield against evil."[6] Keeping memories of wrongdoing alive can protect us from doing that evil again.

By moving beyond the accepted conventions, Jesus turns relating to others upside down. There is a reversal in the process of sharing. Rather than creating a structure through which people could be attracted to church, Jesus began by loving others deeply. Now, structures are necessary, but not if they become more important than people in the church context. In other words, there is something other than personal benefit as the determinant in how relationships begin. What happens is that the usual hierarchical levels in determining relationships are flattened. Jesus moves us beyond the world that we know. By following Jesus, we may find ourselves looking at people of all nations as our equals. Such willingness to bring a radically new way of seeing the world—one of equality—is difficult. We can come to see our world from equality only by having a profound relationship with God and living with that presence in our lives. "Go therefore and make disciples of all nations" can happen only from profound love born in relationship.

Notes

1. Wayne Jackson, "The Publican Factor," *ChristianCourier.com*, https://www.christiancourier.com/articles/897-publican-factor-the.

2. Miroslav Volf, *The End of Memory: Remembering Rightly in a Violent World* (Grand Rapids: Eerdmans, 2006), 26.

3. Sigmund Freud, *The Standard Edition of the Complete Works of Sigmund Freud*, vol. 11, *Five Lectures on Psycho-Analysis* (London: Hogarth, 1955), 19.

4. Miroslav Volf, *The End of Memory: Remembering Rightly in a Violent World* (Grand Rapids: Eerdmans, 2006), 29.

5. Ibid.

6. Elie Wiesel, "Nobel Lecture: Hope, Despair and Memory," December 11, 1986, *Nobelprize.org*, http://www.nobelprize.org/nobel_prizes/peace/laureates/1986/wiesel-lecture.html.

CONCLUSION

Living in a New Home

Love the family of believers. (1 Peter 2:17, NRSV)

In the introduction, I told the story of my church's Pentecost moment at a Christmas Eve service. Our Christmas Eve service now has the same order of worship and the same repertoire of carols that it had when we had our Pentecost moment. At the same time, the service is entirely different than it was on that day. Everything is translated into Spanish in various ways—the printed materials, the text projected on a screen, the electronic information about the service. Another change is that everyone sings the carols in their preferred language. While we sing, images drawn from various cultures depicting the stories from the Scripture lessons serve as the background of our singing or for meditation during the lesson readings. In the years since we had our Pentecost Christmas Eve service, the people listening and recognizing their own language in the event have become part of the planning for subsequent Pentecosts. We are no longer who we were, but that is not because we ceased to be. Instead, we are no longer who we were because we are now so much more, including who we were fully.

The process of settling into our new home has made us keenly aware of how much we benefit from our interdependence. Above all is our relationship with Jesus, but we have formed and have come to value our relationships with one another and others. Some people have made the journey with us from the beginning; and some people are those whom we once saw as "other" but now see as part of our larger family.

Throughout this book, many of the stories have revolved around relationships. My hope is that, as you settle into your new home, those stories will continue to inform your journey. Relationships change and grow over time, but the Word of God and the experience of God's people continue to give insight as new situations or new questions arise.

So, for example, a leader might refer to some of the Scripture passages in this book and use them in traditional ways, such as forming the basis for a sermon series, Bible study, or Christian education workshop. However, the new questions will likely lead to slightly different answers in a new situation.

My further hope is that the stories in the book will serve as examples for churches seeking to discern their next steps. Some steps are comparatively small and simple, such as my church's changing the Christmas Eve worship service by adding a hymn and the living example of a young man placing the baby Jesus in the manger. Others, such as the Filipino and Hungarian congregations sharing a prayer service, call for greater change. Yet, that change was made possible by people having the courage to choose to spend time together over meals or sports events. Those smaller choices led to a larger, significant choice.

If a congregation faces a particularly significant decision, the principles regarding how churches welcome the other in their midst outlined in chapter 5 may again be useful in charting the church's course. Or the steps of recovery and reengagement may again come into play.

In all circumstances, we know that God has been saving God's people for millennia. We are not without hope of guidance; we are called to "grow in the grace and knowledge of our Lord and Savior Jesus Christ. To him be the glory both now and to the day of eternity. Amen" (2 Peter 3:18, NRSV).